See How You Are Loved

MARTHA NELSON

BROADMAN PRESS
Nashville, Tennessee

Unless otherwise noted, all Scripture quotations are taken from the King James Version of the Bible.

Scripture quotations marked GNB are taken from the *Good News Bible,* the Bible in Today's English Version. Old Testament: Copyright © American Bible Society 1976; New Testament: Copyright © American Bible Society 1966, 1971, 1976. Used by permission.

Scripture quotations marked TLB are taken from *The Living Bible.* Copyright © Tyndale House Publishers, Wheaton, Illinois, 1971. Used by permission.

Excerpt from William Barclay on page 36 from *The Letters of John and Jude* Revised Edition. Translated with an Introduction and Interpretation by William Barclay. Revised Edition Copyright © 1976 William Barclay. Published in the U.S.A. by The Westminster Press. Used by permission.

Library of Congress Cataloging-in-Publication Data

Nelson, Martha.
    See how you are loved / Martha Nelson.
        p. cm.
    ISBN 0-8054-5731-3
    1. Christian life—Baptist authors. I. Title.
BV4501.2.N439 1988
248.4'861—dc19   87-18638
                                                                    CIP

Acknowledgments

Words of hymns in public domain are from *The Broadman Hymnal,* Broadman Press; *Baptist Hymnal,* Convention Press; *Hymns for the Family of God,* Paragon Associates, Inc.; or *The Baptist Hymn Book,* Morrison and Gibb Ltd.

"We are the Lord's planting," by Roy Lessin, Dayspring Cards. Used by permission.

"The Lord is my Pace-Setter," from *Psalm 23—An Anthology* by K. H. Strange. Reproduced by kind permission of the Saint Andrew Press, Edinburgh, Scotland.

Prayers by Richard Wong, from *Prayers from an Island,* by Richard Wong. Copyright M. E. Bratcher 1968. Published by John Knox Press. Used by permission.

"Love's Prerogative," by John Oxenham (1852-1941). From *The Best Loved Religious Poems,* James Gilchrist Lawson, compiler. Published by Fleming H. Revell Co. By permission of Desmond Dunkerley.

Excerpts from Gertrude Jekyll, from *Gertrude Jekyll on Gardening,* ed., Penelope Hobhouse, David R. Godine, Publisher.

Excerpts from D. Elton Trueblood, *While It Is Day* by D. Elton Trueblood. Yokefellow Press, 1974.

Ideas on creativity, from *Applied Imagination,* Alex F. Osborn. Charles Scribner's Sons, 1963.

"The Parents' Creed," from *Power Ideas for a Happy Family* by Robert H. Schuller. Copyright © 1972 by Robert Harold Schuller. Published by Fleming H. Revell Co. Used by permission.

"My Neighbor's Roses," by Abraham L. Gruber, from *Best Loved Poems of the American People,* copyright © 1936 Double-

Contents

Part 1

Enjoy the Lord

See how He loves you

1

THE BIG magnolia blossom in the shallow bowl on my desk was an attention-getter. Everyone who passed by stopped to admire it. But Lee, our receptionist, gave it an added dimension of beauty.

"A neighbor brought it late yesterday afternoon," I explained, adding thoughtfully, "Yesterday was such a nice day. Another neighbor came by with a sampling of freshly made crabapple jelly."

Bending close to catch the full, heavy fragrance of the blossom, she said, "See how you are loved, Martha. See how you are loved!"

Long after the blossom faded, Lee's words stayed with me. And magnolia blooms continue to remind me to see how I am loved. Love, you know, is not something you can actually see. You *can* see how love works, however.

See how parents love—see them loving their new baby. Patting, admiring, talking to, rocking, they do everything possible to make their infant comfortable and secure.

See them loving their growing children. Hugging, pleasing, teaching, surprising, disciplining, they reassure them of their love.

See parents loving their teenagers. They transport, help, do without for, and believe in these often-rebellious, assertive youngsters.

See them loving their adult children, lending a hand and sometimes money, ever hoping and praying for their well-being.

See how friends love. They listen, they share, they understand, they stand by one another.

See how teachers and coaches and club leaders love. They respect, encourage, like, and affirm those they lead.

See how God loves. See His creation—the sunshine, the meadows, the redbuds rosy in the woods. See His understanding, His forgiveness, the priceless, superb, superlative Gift He has given for the salvation of all the people of the world. See His mercy and His grace. See the resources He has supplied to help you cope with life, and the peace that passeth all understanding. See the creative potential He has placed within you. See how He ministers to your needs . . . and how He ministers to others through your caring touch.

See how Jesus loves. See His loving-kindness to those whose lives He touched when He walked the paths of Palestine. See His supreme sacrifice. During an Easter drama tears came to my eyes as I watched Him fall under the heavy cross He was bearing. See how you are loved!

Love is so precious; it should never be taken for granted.

It is a good thing to know we are loved. It brings self-confidence, self-respect, a sense of well-being. We are not so self-conscious when we know we are loved. Someone has said you can stand 'most anything when you know that you are loved.

And seeing how we are loved helps us learn how to love. -

See how much the Father has loved us! His love is so great that we are called God's children—and so, in fact, we are. This is why the world does not know us: it has not known God. My dear friends, we are now God's children, but it is not yet clear what we shall become. But we know that when Christ appears, we shall be like him, because we shall see him as he really is. Everyone who has this hope in Christ keeps himself pure, just as Christ is pure (1 John 3:1-3, GNB).

*

2

STRETCHED OUT on the floor of our den, looking out upon the cluster of beautiful pines just beyond our patio, I thought about God.

What is it like, I wondered, *this love of God?* From years of Sunday School classes and sermons I had the facts. But my image of God lacked something. I found myself thinking mostly of Him as a God to satisfy. To be perfectly truthful, I wasn't enjoying being a Christian.

I've been warned that you run into trouble when you start comparing the attributes of God with those of human beings, but that day, lying there on the floor thinking about Him, I ventured in that direction anyhow.

"What's the greatest human love you've experienced?" I asked myself.

"Your husband's," came the answer.

A starting point! My husband does love me very much. He loves me "as is," with all my imperfections. Even on the worst of days.

He made, and has kept, a long-term commitment to me, his wife, just as he promised on our wedding day, "for better, for worse, from this day forward." I don't have to worry about that.

I'm so confident of this human love that I can relax and be myself at home. I enjoy life with my husband.

And why not with God? He created me. He knows my every thought, my every motive, my every deed. He cares about what has happened to me and what is happening. He understands. He loves me "as is," with all my imperfections. Even on the worst of days.

I believe in a loving God now as never before. I know there's far more to God's love than what I discovered that day. But for then it was enough.

That was the day I began to *enjoy* the Lord.

*

3

RECENTLY I read an account of a woman who, like myself, has not always known she could enjoy God. Rejected by her parents, as a child she was an unwanted, ugly little thing who proved to be slow in school and very naughty. Punished, deprived, and certain she was "no good," she ran away from home.

But somewhere along the way she accepted Jesus Christ as her Lord and Savior. She misunderstood what God was like, however. She thought He was loving only when she was obedient and "good," so to speak. The rest of the time she believed Him to be a vengeful and angry God.

More than twenty years passed before her concept of God changed, but thanks to study, classes she attended, and the gentle Christians she came to know, she learned that God is indeed a loving, forgiving, compassionate Father.

Along with this understanding came a new view of herself as a worthwhile person whom God values very highly. She has had to work very hard to replace the inferiority feelings carried over from childhood, but today she basks in the wonderful love of our Heavenly Father.

*

4

I HAVE permission to enjoy God. An old catechism on which many a Christian has cut his teeth has as its beginning statement, "Man's chief end is to glorify God, and to enjoy Him forever."

The Bible is replete with references that encourage us to enjoy our God. For instance, just look at the use of the word *delight.*

As I read Psalm 37, I hear the faraway voices of children in Vacation Bible School repeating together,

Trust in the Lord, and do good: so shalt thou dwell in the land, and verily thou shalt be fed.

Delight thyself also in the Lord; and he shall give thee the desires of thine heart.

Commit thy way unto the Lord; trust also in him; and he shall bring it to pass (vv. 3-5).

Read it aloud for yourself. Look at the promise that hinges upon our delight in the Lord: "the desires of thine heart." Think for a moment—what are the desires of your heart? A small price to pay for those desires dearest to you! Delight thyself in the Lord!

*

5

GOD IS pleased to see us enjoying life. Paul, writing to Timothy, said, "Charge them that are rich in this world, that they be not highminded, nor trust in uncertain riches, but in the living God, who giveth us richly all things to enjoy" (1 Tim. 6:17). He doesn't skimp on His gifts for our pleasure; rather, He is a very generous God. He lavishly provides us with all the joys of life.

The Book of Philippians has been called "The Epistle of Excellent Things" and "The Epistle of Joy." You may want to spend some time reading this lovely letter written by the apostle Paul. Underscore the words *joy* and *rejoice* each time you come across them. Look for the many things that Paul reminds us are our gifts from God, gifts He has given us to enjoy.

Rejoice in the Lord alway: and again I say, Rejoice (Phil. 4:4).

*

6

THE GOOD news of great joy, announced by an angel of the Lord to the shepherds on the night of our Savior's birth, came to me through some love letters from my husband and an ordinary dictionary.

He and I were an idealistic young couple, both church members. From the first evening of our marriage we read from the Bible together. From our first paycheck we contributed generously to the church.

But something was missing, and he was the first to discover that "something." Two thousand miles away, stationed at the Aiea Naval Base in Pearl Harbor, Hawaii, he made the Savior of the world his personal Savior.

I knew from his letters that a great change had come over him, for they suddenly contained line after line of joy in describing his new relationship with God.

Back home with my parents, I realized that besides the mountains and ocean separating us, there was a spiritual chasm. You can imagine my restlessness—the restlessness of physical separation from him, of the late stages of pregnancy, of uncertainty about the future. And now another unrest— would I know this man when he returned? We seemed to have so little in common.

But it was another restlessness, the dawning realization that I lacked a personal relationship with God, that started me on my search for joy.

The search involved a close examination of myself, of my understanding as to what being a Christian was all about. It led to questions, even doubts, about the divinity of Jesus Christ. It forced me to an intellectual examination of His life as recorded in the four Gospels. And it ended with the realization that the heart does not find itself in God by gracious deeds or mere mental assent.

That's where the dictionary came in. "For by grace are ye saved through faith; and that not of yourselves: it is the gift of God: Not of works, lest any man should boast," my husband wrote.

Reading Ephesians 2:8-9, I went to the family dictionary for meanings I'd somehow failed to grasp in years of sermons:

Grace: an unmerited, undeserved gift; a favor rendered by one who need not do so; divine love and protection freely bestowed upon mankind.

Faith: a confident belief in the truth, value, or trustworthiness of a person, idea, or thing; belief that does not rest on logical proof or material evidence; loyalty to a person or thing.

Back to his letter, I reread the verses: "For by an unmerited, undeserved act on the part of a loving God, I can be saved by a confident belief in the truth, value, and trustworthiness of Jesus Christ as my Savior."

In silent prayer I reviewed the sin in my life, sought God's forgiveness, and reached up to Him in earnestness, with my whole being.

And there I found the Joy, the joy of salvation, the beginning place of joy.

*

7

CALL IT the new birth, being saved or born again, this divine happening is not easy to explain. Our Lord said it was like the wind which, though you can't see it, is positively there.

I think it is like finding the home of your dreams and moving in. . . . Like being homesick and going home. . . . Like being confined by illness and finally released. . . . Like being a stunted plant, out of its natural environment, suddenly put into the warm earth where it can respond to sunlight and fresh air and rainfall.

It is the beginning of a "new you."

It is belonging.

It is being loved—and you know you can stand almost anything so long as you know you're loved.

It is self-respect, a reassurance of your worth.

It is a settled mind, a this-is-it feeling.

It is an ancient set of values suddenly become valuable to you.

It is support which works when nothing else can.

It is a peace of mind defying all human understanding.

And it is joy—the reward of a solid, settled relationship with God.

I will greatly rejoice in the Lord, my soul shall be joyful in my God; for he hath clothed me with the garments of salvation, he hath covered me with the robe of righteousness, as a bridegroom decketh himself with ornaments, and as a bride adorneth herself with her jewels (Isa. 61:10).

*

8

I CALL it my "first morning," the morning after I committed my life to Jesus Christ as my Savior and Lord. I recall so vividly going out in the backyard of my parents' home, where I was staying while my husband was overseas, to hang diapers on the clothesline.

The world never looked more beautiful, the trees greener, the freshness of the air never more pleasant. It was a mere moment of joy but one that remains sharply etched in my memory.

It is an added joy to know that here and there others have been aware of a similar newness. It confirms for me the reality of the new birth when I know that a poet by the name of George Wade Robinson who lived in England in the 1800s experienced the very feelings I had on my "first morning":

> Heav'n above is softer blue,
>> Earth around is sweeter green;
> Something lives in ev'ry hue,
>> Christless eyes have never seen:
> Birds with gladder songs o'erflow,
>> Flow'rs with deeper beauties shine,
> Since I know, as now I know,
>> I am his and he is mine.

*

9

ONCE IN a while since my "first morning" I experience a similar heightened awareness of God's creation. It happened again on a late afternoon walk with my husband in the beautiful Shaw's Gardens in St. Louis. He had come for me at my office for a little date during one of those many weeks when we had to search for time alone together.

Scarcely anyone was in sight at that hour of the day, just before closing time. It was too early in the season for the tourists, who linger to catch every moment of beauty in a crowded schedule, and the gardeners were probably putting away their tools.

The late afternoon sun, the same sun Adam and Eve were warmed by, cast long shadows, leaving glints of golden light in shining splotches here and there. A great oak stretched its sheltering arms above us. The weedless flower beds offered beauty for the taking.

"It's like the Garden of Eden," I exclaimed, hating to break the silence which was almost as lovely as the loveliness that surrounded us, ". . . everything is so perfect."

Places and moments like that are made for the enjoyment of God, and I'm thankful for people with vision who provide them for us.

*

10

WITHOUT A settled relationship with God, it is impossible to enjoy Him. No two of us come to faith in exactly the same way, or under exactly the same circumstances, but too often we have heard well-meaning Christians draw hard-and-fast conclusions that faith will come to others only as it has come to them.

Yet we have all known those who were reared in Christian homes and in the context of the church, to whom faith came almost as quietly and naturally as any ordinary birthday.

Others experienced highly dramatic encounters with God which brought them face to face with their sin and turned them around abruptly.

Some look back to a simple experience of faith as a child, which they later affirmed as a youth who understood far more fully the meaning of following the Lord.

The test of faith, I'm convinced, is our relationship and commitment to the Lord Jesus Christ and His church.

John the apostle wrote the letter we call First John for the express purpose of reassuring believers, "that ye may know that ye have eternal life, and that ye may believe on the name of the Son of God" (5:13).

The Spirit itself beareth witness with our spirit, that we are the children of God (Rom. 8:16).

And hereby we do know that we know him, if we keep his commandments (1 John 2:3).

We know that we have passed from death unto life, because we love the brethren (1 John 3:14a).

And hereby we know that he abideth in us, by the Spirit which he hath given us (1 John 3:24b).

Hereby know we that we dwell in him, and he in us, because he hath given us of his Spirit (1 John 4:13).

Whosoever shall confess that Jesus is the Son of God, God dwelleth in him, and he in God (1 John 4:15).

Whosoever believeth that Jesus is the Christ is born of God (1 John 5:1a).

*

11

RIGHT AFTER Christmas each year the seed catalogs start arriving. Gardening season has begun! First there's the browsing through, just looking. Then in a couple of weeks my husband, the gardener, gets down to serious business. Spreading the catalogs out on the dining table, with last year's order close by, he makes up his order for seeds.

My comments usually run, "We won't eat that much corn, or all those beets!"

"But you have to plant for the animals, too, and then there are the kids and our friends. We need some to give away," he always replies.

He wins out, of course.

Next thing we know he's out plowing and tilling. The seeds arrive, and my husband disappears. He loves working with the soil.

He believes man has an affinity for soil because it was from the dust of the earth that the Lord God formed the first man.

Whatever the reason, folks like to dabble in the dirt, trying their hand at growing vegetables.

God must enjoy planting the seeds of faith in our lives and watching them sprout and grow and produce. Our spiritual development must bring Him joy, just as gardening brings joy to so many people.

In fact, the prophet Isaiah speaks of the house of Israel as "the vineyard of the Lord, . . . and the men of Judah his pleasant plant" (Isa. 5:7).

We are the Lord's planting.
He watches over us with
great care and detail.
He nourishes us, sustains us, and
causes us to blossom.
It is the fragrance and fruitfulness
of our lives that bring forth praise
to Him, our husbandman.

—Roy Lessin

*

12

FOR MANY years September has been a magical month for me. September marked the beginning of school, and I liked school. I liked the new books and the fresh school supplies, the new clothes, the new friends, the new teacher.

I liked the invigorating feel of early fall days. The anticipation of new experiences was exhilarating.

As our children grew into their school years I enjoyed helping them get ready and off to school. It had a settling effect on our family. The routine was good for us all.

Autumn's golden days remind me it's time to wrap up another summer and get set for a new season. As my garden year winds down, the Great Gardener goes on about His business of painting the world with great splashes of color upon the trees.

But September beginnings, glorious as they are, just don't compare with the everyday beginnings God has provided His children. "Then he separated the light from the darkness, and he named the light Day and the darkness Night. Evening passed and morning came—that was the first day" (Gen. 1:4-5, GNB).

Thank God that He divided time into days and nights. Thank God for every beginning. Life would be unbearable otherwise.

*

13

A MUTUAL interest is a sure-fire basis for friendship. Visiting my aging mother, I was repeatedly amazed at the number of friends and acquaintances she acquired through her interest in plants and flowers.

People were constantly calling and coming by to show and tell what was happening in their yards and gardens. Others arrived, spade in hand, to get a start of her day lilies. There was scarcely a dull moment.

When you share a strong interest with another person, things like age, appearance, education, and social standing lose their importance. You become absorbed in sharing. The shallower the interest, the more these superficial matters seem to interfere.

Fortunate is the person who begins early in life to develop a hobby or strong interest. It may be sewing, writing, painting, or any one of a myriad of crafts or collections; or it may be a cause like missions or Scouting or some special community service.

While the mental or physical activity involved in your hobby or cause is rewarding, never underestimate its potential for friendships.

And consider the friendships that develop through your church. God is good to have put people together, not only in families but in churches as well. There may be a few flawed saints among us, but by and large you'll find some of God's most beautiful creations among the people of the churches that dot the landscape of the world.

Take Mrs. Summer, for instance, a godly woman if ever I met one. She was faithful in her longtime career as a math teacher, faithful to her terminally ill husband, for whom she cared for years, faithful to her friends and acquaintances (she never met a person she didn't respect or like), faithful to her church.

Or Mr. and Mrs. Tims, a gentle, refined, Christlike couple who loved their church, the people of their town, their pastor and his family.

Or John and Gladys Burney, who made services to aging persons their careers and who continue to serve the aging as volunteers in their retirement.

And then there's Buster and Elsie, Steve and Linda, Bill and Elba, and a host of other couples in the fellowship of believers, dear hearts and gentle people who have blessed us so with their friendship.

Think of some of God's beautiful people whom you know. Don't you enjoy the fact that God has peopled the world with so much beauty?

> *Blest be the tie that binds*
> *Our hearts in Christian love;*
> *The fellowship of kindred minds*
> *Is like to that above.*
> —*John Fawcett*

*

14

AT A Little Britches Rodeo in Littleton, Colorado, we got acquainted with an enthusiastic spectator who was getting on up in years.

"Now if that rider had just done this or that," she'd say as the barrel races were run. "There, yonder, is a future rodeo star!"

Between all the exciting events she told us of growing up on a Grand Mesa ranch. On a Saturday afternoon, she reminisced, the men would pull wagons up into a circle where she and other young people did their tricks.

"Do you still ride?" my husband asked.

"No, not any more. Now I just clap!"

Seeing others saved and growing is cause for clapping, too. No doubt you have rejoiced, as the Savior does, on seeing individuals make a public commitment of their faith in Him.

My heart claps, too, as I observe children in church—little girls growing into the women of the church, wiggly boys who are likely to become tomorrow's community leaders, men and women coming to Christ out of the most Christless backgrounds, young adults developing as church leaders.

We enjoy God when we enjoy, along with Him, the work of the Holy Spirit in the lives of others.

*

15

SHE WAS a gracious, attractive woman but she had a multitude of personal problems. Her family was torn apart by separation and a pending divorce. One of her sons was addicted to drugs. They were people who seemingly wanted for nothing, yet lacked so much that I value most highly.

I was shocked when she told me how she still resented the church of her youth. "I felt so restricted," she said. "It wasn't for me."

She didn't have a very good word for any church.

"My church was good for a teenager like me," I countered. "It protected me at a time when I needed protection!"

Here on a windy hill in Oklahoma I am constantly reminded of the value of protection. Right after our move I attempted to recreate a scene similar to my backyard in Mississippi, where a dozen baskets of plants hung beneath our sheltered patio and the surrounding pines.

But the hot southeasterly winds make this kind of gardening virtually impossible. Instead, I'm learning to rely on zinnias and periwinkles and marigolds for color in the unprotected places. Tender plants go into a bed on the east, sheltered from the wind and the afternoon sun.

A great many people, like plants, thrive best in protected places. They grow best in a sheltered environment.

We can rejoice in God's protecting commandments, His guidelines for life, the security of salvation through His Son, "in whom is life everlasting." We can enjoy God's protection.

He that dwelleth in the secret place of the most High shall abide under the shadow of the Almighty.

I will say of the Lord, He is my refuge and my fortress: my God; in him will I trust.

Surely he shall deliver thee from the snare of the fowler, and from the noisome pestilence.

He shall cover thee with his feathers, and under his wings shalt thou trust: his truth shall be thy shield and buckler (Ps. 91:1-4).

*

16

WALKING TO breakfast on a spring day during a writers' conference in Birmingham, I passed one of those lovely old churchyard gardens you'll find here and there in American cities. Behind the dark wrought iron fence azaleas bloomed brightly. A bricked path led to a little fountain. Daffodils peeked through the fence as if to say, "Good morning!"

As it started to sprinkle, I ducked into a coffee shop. The cashier was pleasant, and as I started to complain about the weather, she replied in a slow, sweet drawl, "It's just a mawnin' rain, ma'am!"

I've enjoyed many a "mawnin' rain" since. Thank God for folks who recognize God's benefits for what they really are and share their insights with others. Words from a hymn by J. W. Chadwick express it so well:

> And thanks for the harvest of beauty,
>   For that which the hands cannot hold,
> The harvest eyes only can gather,
>   And only our hearts can enfold.

For, lo, the winter is past, the rain is over and gone; The flowers appear on the earth; the time of the singing of birds is come (Song of Sol. 2:11-12).

*

17

WHEN EVERYTHING'S going your way it's easy to rejoice. Great, wonderful, fantastic: we search for superlatives.

But what about when things are not so good? When nothing seems to be in your favor?

Emogene Harris, a missionary to Nigeria, told me of an elderly African Christian, Madame Susannah, who knew how to rejoice in the Lord even in the worst of circumstances.

Evacuated from her home during a terrible civil war, she wandered from one refugee camp to another, almost starving to death at times. There were times when she thought she would surely die in a bombing.

Finally, after many months, she returned home to find her house just a shell, her beloved church badly damaged, her city half-destroyed.

"God saw me through," she told Miss Harris. She rejoiced in spite of her circumstances.

Asked if she had a message for Christians in America, Madame Susannah pointed to the tattered Bible she carried throughout the war and said, "Tell them to study the Bible every day. It is the Food of Life."

Yet I will rejoice in the Lord, I will joy in the God of my salvation (Hab. 3:18).

Thy Word is like a garden, Lord,
    With flowers bright and fair;
And ev'ry one who seeks may pluck
    A lovely garland there.

Thy Word is like a deep, deep mine;
    And jewels rich and rare
Are hidden in its mighty depths,
    For ev'ry searcher there.

Thy Word is like a starry host;
    A thousand rays of light
Are seen, to guide the traveler
    And make his pathway bright.

Thy Word is like a glorious choir,
    And loud its anthems ring;
Though many tongues and parts unite,
    It is one song they sing.

O may I love Thy precious Word,
    May I explore the mine,
May I its fragrant flowers glean,
    May light upon me shine.
                    — Edwin Hodder

*

18

I WAS out-of-doors yesterday morning, a cool April morning, removing spent blossoms from irises, pruning a dead tip from a shrub here and there, moving dirt and smoothing the ground along the strip of brick we have laid as a retainer for a foundation planting. A light breeze was blowing. It was invigorating to be outside, moving about, breathing deeply of the clean fresh air.

Such activity seems to have a cleansing effect on body, mind, and spirit. When I pace myself and don't hurry through or stay at it too long, I find it most refreshing.

There's a cleansing that comes, also, when we ask God's forgiveness of the sins we've committed. Our loving God stands ready to forgive and, the Bible says, to cleanse us of all unrighteousness.

Inevitably, our hearts will condemn us at times. But we have a God who is "greater than our heart, and knoweth all things" (1 John 3:20).

"Not only does he know our sins," William Barclay reminds us, "he also knows our love, our longings, the nobility that never fully works itself out, our penitence; and the greatness of his knowledge gives him the sympathy which can understand and forgive. . . . Men can judge us only by our actions, but God can judge us by the longings which never became deed and the dreams which never came true. . . . The perfect knowledge which belongs to God, and to God alone, is not our terror but our hope."

Joy is knowing you are forgiven and all's well between you and the Lord.

Happy are those whose sins are forgiven,
  whose wrongs are pardoned.
Happy is the man
  whom the Lord does not accuse of doing wrong
  and who is free from all deceit.

You that are righteous, be glad and rejoice
  because of what the Lord has done.
You that obey him, shout for joy! (Ps. 32:1-2, 11, GNB).

*

19

A CHRISTIAN'S journey is marked by many revelations that result in joy in the Lord. Like the stepping-stones we've laid which invite us to come and enjoy at close hand some of God's handiwork, these revelations invite us to move forward in a life of joy in the Lord.

For joy comes with a growing understanding of who God is, what He is like and how we may honor and obey Him.

As a young Christian I was under the impression that God's will had to do only with big decisions, major turning points, in our lives.

"Oh, no," my friend Sue explained. "God is interested in your everyday decisions, too."

This was a major stepping-stone along my path toward Christian maturity. After all, life goes on, a day at a time. Major decisions usually are few and far between. And if we don't watch out, one day we'll find that life has happened, as someone has said, while we're making other plans.

Some of us wander through life aimlessly; others live "intentionally." Drawing aside daily for prayer and planning can make all the difference.

"How shall I relate to my spouse, my supervisor on the job, my colleagues, my neighbors? How can I best help my children at this point in time? How should I use my time?"

Meditation, prayer, and the study of the Bible help us to access the answers. Joy comes in the assurance that we are trying, with the help of the Holy Spirit, to live according to the will of God. For truly, as the psalmist reminds us, "The statutes of the Lord are right, rejoicing the heart" (Ps. 19:8).

When we walk with the Lord
  In the light of his Word,
What a glory he sheds on our way!
  Let us do His good will,
He abides with us still,
  And with all who will trust and obey.

Trust and obey,
  for there's no other way
To be happy in Jesus,
  but to trust and obey.

— *J. H. Sammis*

*

20

REMEMBER THE story Jesus told of the servants who were given the talents, one five, another two, and another one? Entrusting the three servants with his money, their master left them in charge and departed for a far country.

On his return he was delighted to find that the servant to whom he had entrusted the five talents had doubled them. He affirmed this servant: "Well done . . . enter thou into the joy of thy lord" (Matt. 25:21).

The second servant, likewise, had done well with the two talents. And likewise, the master affirmed him: "Enter thou into the joy of thy lord" (v. 23).

The third, sad to say, had hidden his single talent—out of fear, he declared, lest it be lost and his master angered. But he had misjudged his master! Instead of praise, he received a severe reprimand for not investing it as the others had done.

God expects us to be productive with the resources He entrusts to us. Note the reward in store for the productive servants: "Enter thou into the joy of thy Lord." An invitation to joy—His joy.

Our Lord's joy has a dimension that transcends our normal responses to the passing pleasures of life. It is a vicarious experience, entered into with One we love. It is a deep and abiding sense of well-being, an assurance that all is well. It is a peace that passeth all understanding.

*

Part 2

Value Serenity

*See the resources a loving God supplies
for coping with the strains and stresses of life*

WE DON'T talk a lot about serenity, yet we most certainly know when it's absent from our lives.

"You wouldn't believe this morning!" we gasp, arriving late at the office.

"Jim's job is shaky," we confide with dark looks and fear in our voices.

"I don't know what's happening to our son . . . I'm concerned about him."

"I'll go stir crazy if I have to look at these four walls much longer!"

And, threateningly, "If another thing goes wrong. . . ."

Serenity is an elusive quality these days. To experience quietness and calmness, to feel inner contentment and a sense of well-being, to have peace of mind in our troubled, broken world is no easy achievement.

Several years ago, in response to my own need and the needs many of my friends had for a better way of life, I explored some of the normal, negative emotions we were experiencing. Surely there are answers, I thought, to these problems which were dissipating our strength and vitality. And so I went in search of ways we might react more effectively to the inevitable strains of responsible living.

I came away from my search marveling at the resources for coping our God has supplied. Often, however, we fail to apply them to daily living.

Jesus is the supreme example of a serene life-style. From childhood He knew who He was, what His purpose in life was, where He was going. He led a life on the road without the usual comforts of home and family. He was frequently disdained and rejected, a prophet without honor in his own hometown. Yet, reading His life and especially the account of His death, we are impressed with His calmness and tranquillity.

To live like that—what a challenge!

22

LIFE DOESN'T have to be so hectic! So the house looks like a cyclone hit it . . . the family is out of sorts . . . the boss needs that misplaced file *yesterday* . . . some of your help on that volunteer project has fallen by the wayside.

Big problems you believe you can handle; it's the little upsets that can ruin a day. "[It's] the little foxes, that spoil the vines" (Song of Sol. 2:15).

The question is, how do you reinforce your fences against those little foxes that constantly threaten your serenity?

One friend recommends seven minutes with God. She takes her seven minutes for meditation and prayer before launching out into her day.

People who drive to work alone sometimes use driving time for drawing nigh. They listen to tapes or a devotional program on the car radio. Or they simply pray.

Others keep devotional material in their desk drawer at work and take a few moments before their day gets under way or during a break to draw nigh.

A gardener draws nigh, kneeling upon the warm earth, pulling weeds.

A quiet time with God can help us develop a customarily good mood, a good disposition. It can sweeten, purify, and transform. It can engender love—patient, kind, gentle love, love that is not easily upset. Confronted with love, the people and events of a day are not so likely to provoke, irritate, exasperate, and anger us.

In this quiet time the Word of God speaks to our need for self-control. It teaches us to live around things which displease, disturb, and disquiet us. Gradually the wisdom of the Word becomes a way of life.

Then, when a spouse is hard to live with or a co-worker is next to impossible, we can test the teaching that "A soft answer turneth away wrath" (Prov. 15:1).

When we're tempted to let our dispositions degenerate into ill humor, we recall, "A merry heart doeth good like a medicine" (Prov. 17:22).

When we feel like lashing out at a family member, "As ye would that men should do to you, do ye . . . likewise" (Luke 6:31) floats up from somewhere in our subconscious. And the fruit of the Spirit called self-control goes on maturing.

Great peace have they which love thy law; and nothing shall offend them (Ps. 119:165).

*

23

IF YOU'RE a busy person with a tendency to overplan, try keeping a calendar along with your daily devotional materials.

I'm so thankful for the Christian writer from whom I learned to bring my planning into my time with God. For years I have kept several calendars, one over my desk, one by the telephone, one in my handbag, and another with my devotional materials. During my prayer time on Monday I take a hard look at what's ahead for the week. Then each morning I look again at what's ahead. My firm commitments are there in black and white. The meetings I will attend, the appointments I have, the promises to keep. That time is taken. I set it aside.

So much physical, mental, and emotional energy will be required. I know from past experience I'd better allow for the unexpected. I consider family commitments which require transportation and other help that takes time. I change my mind about some things that need to be done. This can wait another week. That is not a priority item.

Planning is basic to well-ordered living. Planning, with God's help, can make the difference between "frantic" and "serene." But, as someone has said, "Don't get so organized that you become inflexible and incapable of enjoying life's spontaneous moments. Unpredictable moments enliven and enrich our relationships."

Dear Lord and Father of mankind,
Forgive our foolish ways;
Reclothe us in our rightful mind;
In purer lives thy service find,
In deeper rev'rence, praise.

In simple trust like theirs who heard,
Beside the Syrian sea,
The gracious calling of the Lord,
Let us, like them, without a word,
Rise up and follow thee.

Drop thy still dews of quietness,
Till all our strivings cease;
Take from our souls the strain and stress,
And let our ordered lives confess
The beauty of thy peace.

Breathe thro' the heats of our desire
Thy coolness and thy balm;
Let sense be dumb, let flesh retire;
Speak thro' the earthquake, wind, and fire,
O still small voice of calm!
                    — John Greenleaf Whittier

*

24

RECENTLY WE spent a morning re-laying the flagstones around the birdbath. We had put them there rather hastily several years ago after planting some tulip bulbs, and mowing around the bed was practically impossible. Now that they are level with the ground we can cut the grass far more easily.

Next to the birdbath we've planted day lilies, a glory to behold, starting in May. Beyond these and the tulips, I usually plant pansies in the fall; they begin to bloom a bit in February and keep right on until the weather gets hot. (Pansies are lovely floating in a low dish; it takes only two or three, with violet leaves, to make a lovely little centerpiece for the breakfast table.) While these are still in bloom, I add a circle of summer annuals, this year dwarf marigolds.

This little round garden reminds me that the Christian life is like a circle. At its center is you, and within you are Christ and the Holy Spirit. All around you are your various relationships and responsibilities—your spouse, your children, your church, your job, your extended family, your neighborhood, the world. Add to these "yourself," for you have that responsibility, too.

At times your children may need your full attention, at times your spouse. At a given time you may be heavily involved with a church project and you neglect other things to get the job done. An aging parent may need your care, and you drop all else. Adult children call and you fly across the country, setting aside other responsibilities for a while. A neighbor experiences a crisis and you are there to help out. Your job, when you're working, demands your full attention.

Priorities? They vary from day to day, even hour to hour. But with Christ at the center, He can be first always, regardless of where you turn your attention.

Being a Christian is more than doing "church work." It is sorting out the needs at hand and meeting them, "as unto the Lord." No need to feel guilty because you cannot be all things to all people and everywhere at once!

Serenity is knowing as you serve others that you serve the Lord Christ. It is relaxing to realize that God has the clearest possible view of the circle of our lives. He knows the heart of that person in the center.

*

"OH, TO be in England now that April's there . . ." Truly, every daffodil and tulip in the land—and there must have been millions—appeared to be in bloom when we were there one April.

Early during our stay we learned from our hosts that what we call a "yard" they call their "garden." And tiny though most of them were compared to our American yards, they were simply lovely.

Riding the double-decker buses, we enjoyed looking down on the gardens in many areas of London. The designs were endless, and most were very well kept. In some we noticed that every inch of earth was under cultivation. Everywhere there were flowers, leaving very little grass to mow.

If only we could ride a double-decker now and then to get a new perspective of the garden of our lives! But we're usually so close to what's going on we don't see the pattern, the plan, the patchwork of color which gives it a unique design.

That's why vacations, conferences, and retreats are helpful. A worship service, or some time alone in prayer, also may provide the perspective we need to go back to our routines with renewed vitality.

And everything goes so much better when we don't lose sight of the "big picture" of our lives.

To every thing there is a season,
and a time to every purpose under the heaven:
A time to be born, and a time to die;
a time to plant, and a time to pluck up
that which is planted;
A time to kill, and a time to heal;
a time to break down, and a time to build up;
A time to weep, and a time to laugh;
a time to mourn, and a time to dance;
A time to cast away stones,
and a time to gather stones together;
a time to embrace,
and a time to refrain from embracing;
A time to get,
and a time to lose;
a time to keep,
and a time to cast away;
A time to rend,
and a time to sew;
a time to keep silence,
and a time to speak;
A time to love,
and a time to hate;
a time of war,
and a time of peace
(Eccl. 3:1-8).

*

26

THE BOTANY professor and his wife with whom we stayed overnight in Camberley, a suburb of London, showed us around their garden on Sunday morning before leaving for church. We admired the well-kept flower beds and looked into the several greenhouses, and then he said, "Now let's go up front."

There he pointed out his "wild garden," an uncultivated area beneath tall, ancient trees which has been left to nature's choices.

Should he visit us, I would show him our meadow. I'm indebted to the garden writer who wisely advised, "If you have large areas around your home, consider leaving some of them as they are—in their natural state."

Since then, I've begun to "think meadow." In early spring the area south of the house is blanketed with white, then yellow, and we delight in the assortment of wild flowers scattered here and there.

Toward summertime, as the meadow grows shabby, reluctantly, finally, I allow the meadow to be mowed. But on the rise in the distance we leave clumps of yucca, cacti, and tall native grasses as an accent the year around.

So often we fail to capitalize on what we have at hand. We want to give a city look to a country place. We want to appear to be something we are not. We put on airs.

And serenity is sacrificed in the process.

*

HOW MANY pictures of patience can you visualize in sixty seconds?

Patience is a man and his son fishing beside a sunlit lake.

Patience is a mother at the sewing machine ripping out a mistake.

Patience is a working woman serving an irate customer.

Patience is an anxious parent refusing to give up on a wayward daughter.

Patience is an aging person accepting the changes the years have brought.

Patience is a pastor faithfully preaching without immediate and obvious results.

Patience is a gardener waiting for flowers and vegetables.

Patience is God waiting for His people to prove their love.

Patience is a godly quality. According to Paul's incomparable description in 1 Corinthians 13, it is one facet of love. "[Love] suffereth long" (v. 4).

In his letter to the Galatian Christians, Paul listed patience as a fruit of the Spirit. It is not a spiritual *gift* bestowed by God; rather it is a fruit of the Spirit, developing and maturing as we abide in Christ.

Peter included it in those qualities we should diligently add to our faith. Patience is a vital aspect of serenity. Value patience—it's part of the growth process.

*

28

WE HAVE tried for several years to develop a strawberry bed. A friend gave us dozens of fine, healthy plants. Hastening to get them in the ground, we worked by the light of a full moon, our eyes gradually adjusting to the growing darkness.

We lost those plants to Bermuda grass. Ambitious to grow everything we'd ever heard of, we found ourselves with a whole lot more than we could care for.

Second time around, it was a very hot dry summer, and maybe we waited too late in the season to plant. Whatever the cause, we lost those, too.

This time we've planted in a tiered bed, confining the plants with strips of metal, locating the bed near a hydrant where watering will be no problem.

"Pinch off all blossoms the first season," the instructions read. "Let the growth go into the plants rather than fruit."

Likewise, our asparagus bed went untouched the first two years, according to instructions, "Don't harvest right away." So we waited, and sure enough this spring we began to enjoy a plentiful yield of those tender, delicious spears.

Nobody really likes delays. Yet it takes time for some of our efforts to pay off. Serenity is being willing to make a sacrifice in favor of a long-term gain.

*

I'VE HAD to learn the hard way to admit my limitations. In my initial enthusiasm for gardening I kept adding places to plant the many varieties of flowers that looked so appealing in the catalogs and garden books.

"A bed would be lovely here . . . or there," I'd say to my husband. "Get the tiller and let's get started."

Great ideas, yes, but I didn't have the time and energy to take care of them. Again, that Bermuda grass was my downfall! Just couldn't keep it out!

When the phone would ring and I knew guests were on their way, not only did I have to get the house in order and make preparation for meals, also I had to rush out and frantically neaten up those flower beds.

Well, you guessed it. I'm cutting back. Dug a bushel of irises and countless galliardias and daisies, plus some bulbs last fall. I put the irises down near The Forest, near enough to enjoy the blooms, far enough away not to worry about weeds and grass. Naturalizing, the garden experts call it. Had lots to give away.

Admitting your limitations is not easy. Sometimes there's no way to save face. You just have to say, "I've undertaken more than I can possibly handle. This is the straw that breaks the camel's back."

But don't pick a "down" day to make your decision. Give yourself time to decide. How much time and energy are you willing to expend, how much do you have to expend, how much value do you place on a given task? Is it a short-term project you can manage to see to completion, or is it long-term?

Serenity is taking charge of your life, admitting your limitations and choosing, sometimes by trial and error, what you're going to do with it.

*

30

IN A recent conference I asked the participants to close their eyes and recall a scene from the life of Jesus. It was a precious time, hearing one after another share how they remembered Him in that moment—

. . . blessing children

. . . healing lepers

. . . praying in the Garden

. . . carrying His cross

. . . teaching on a mountainside

. . . walking with the two on the Emmaus road

. . . preparing breakfast for His disciples one early morning beside the sea.

We don't have to wait for the observance of the Lord's Supper to spend time in remembrance of Him. Indeed, it would be a good practice to stop and consciously recall a memory of our Lord at least once a day.

A meaningful memory is a precious blessing. "God has given us memories that we may have roses in December," wrote James Barrie.

Take time to consciously remember Jesus, especially during your bleaker times. Remember His power . . . His wisdom . . . His purity . . . His suffering . . . His death . . . His resurrection . . . His return.

Tell me the stories of Jesus
I love to hear;
Things I would ask Him to tell me
If He were here.
Scenes by the wayside,
Tales of the sea,
Stories of Jesus,
Tell them to me.
— *William H. Parker*

*

31

SOON AFTER buying our place we planted a dozen dwarf fruit trees—apple, pear, peach, and plum—and it's amazing how they've grown in a few years.

Late in winter, or very early spring (however you wish to think of it), a friend has come to prune them for us. Pruning is such a painful process for novice gardeners like ourselves; it hurts to clip away those branches. But everything we read says it must be done, and we trust our friend. He's the unofficial pruner in the community—got his experience working for the Stark Nursery.

When he arrives, we go down to the orchard to watch closely as he carefully examines each branch and as carefully performs the surgery.

Just as pruning shapes a shrub or tree, the painful experiences that come to every believer serve to shape us up. At the time we agonize, we wonder why, we don't understand.

"What happened took something out of me," we reflect. But, given time, we come to realize—eventually—that good can come out of difficulty, and spiritual growth can result. Healing occurs, and we know we can endure other difficulties now as never before.

Our love for God, our reliance on Him, and our faith in His sustaining power is stronger because we've undergone some pruning, some shaping, some tidying up.

We know the peace that passeth all understanding. Pruning brings forth the fruit of the Spirit—love, peace, faith, meekness, and yes, even joy.

I will extol thee, O Lord;
for thou hast lifted me up,
and hast not made my foes to rejoice over me.
O Lord my God, I cried unto thee,
and thou hast healed me.
O Lord, thou hast brought up my soul from the grave:
thou hast kept me alive,
that I should not go down to the pit.
Sing unto the Lord, O ye saints of his,
and give thanks
at the remembrance of his holiness.
For his anger endureth but a moment;
in his favour is life:
weeping may endure for a night,
but joy cometh in the morning (Ps. 30:1-5).

*

32

"NEVER SATISFIED!" we say sometimes about someone who is a chronic grumbler. And we ourselves may occasionally go through periods of discontent.

Of course, not all discontent is bad. Someone has spoken of the "splendid discontent" of God with the formless void from which He created the universe. Progress depends upon people who are not satisfied with the status quo.

But negative discontent is a misery which afflicts far too many people. I recall a time in my life when I was going through a period of discontent. Our two older daughters were home from college for the summer, and our high schooler was "around the house." The older girls had been fortunate enough to find summer jobs, and I was continuing to hold down my job at school, with reduced hours, in order to help meet college expenses. My husband's demanding profession had not let up one iota in consideration of this busy time in our family's life.

We lived next door to the church, and between the doorbell and knocks at the basement entrance, the telephone, stereo, piano, TV, and radio—well, to say the least, it was all beginning to tell on me!

For days I had awakened bad-humoredly, inexcusably cross with my family.

Then one morning I found on the bulletin board near our breakfast table these hand-printed words, placed there by our eldest daughter:

"How beautiful a day can be when kindness touches it."

One miserable woman saw herself that morning and determined to get control of herself. It marked a turning point in my life.

We use self-control to achieve in so many situations. A cook, baking a pie, doesn't haphazardly throw unmeasured ingredients together, just hoping a mouth-watering dessert will result. A secretary rolling stationery into her typewriter exercises control in turning out a perfect letter. A doctor knows good patient care doesn't just happen; he or she controls results by following definite procedures. A teacher plans for a controlled learning situation so the class can move toward established goals. A good salesperson exerts control and care in displaying merchandise and dealing with customers.

But how often we fail to master, to control, our personal response to disturbing circumstances. We neglect personal self-control. And then we wonder why life is not serene.

*

33

OVER THE past four years we have planted several hundred seedlings provided by our state forestry department. Many were little more than a stubby switch with a wisp of a root when we put them into the earth. Yet some of the cedars already stand five feet tall, the black locusts are twice that height, and the lacebark elms are developing into lovely little trees.

Likewise, the dogwood which came from the National Arbor Day Foundation is at last beginning to look like a dogwood.

We plant seeds and get corn on the cob for our dinner table. I send away for rose bushes, and the bare roots which arrive in the mail soon produce lush foliage and beautiful roses.

Miracles of God! There are so many things in life that can only be explained in terms of God. And they are happening all about us every day of our lives. "The earth is full of miracles for the eye that sees," Barclay has written.

Some speak of luck, others fate. But those to whom God is real see His hand at work. What some would call a twist of circumstance, the believer sees as an answer to prayer.

I have been reading the Gospels lately and have been impressed more than ever before with the number of incidents where Jesus healed those who were handicapped or ill. Maybe it's because of the devastating news that our daughter has cancer, and my mind even at rest is concerned with her healing.

Her physicians made it very plain—they will do all in their power—but ultimately healing lies in the power of God.

Reading how Jesus healed when He was here on earth gives

me hope. And so I pray for another miracle. I believe in miracles. How about you?

> *O sing unto the Lord a new song;*
> *for he hath done marvellous things (Ps. 98:1).*

*

34

THE MOST mail I've ever received from readers came in response to a little devotional in *Open Windows* on the subject of self-control. In it I shared how the very day I began serious work on the series I lost my temper.

We had just moved, and my husband was looking for something, I can't recall just what. And, as has been par for the course for many years, he implied that I might have discarded it in the move.

You see, many years ago I *had* discarded something which should have been kept. And he has never let me forget it! It's obvious that his self-control is tested when he cannot find something he needs right now.

I was weary from the move, and it didn't take much to upset me that day. And what a loss—it practically ruined my entire day.

Most of us run into times of testing, and we don't always score 100 percent. It's our loss when tempers flare, for every minute we're angry we lose sixty seconds of happiness. Accusations are made which cannot be recalled, efficiency is affected, time is wasted, our sense of well-being is destroyed for a while.

How good it is to realize that self-control is a fruit of the Spirit and that God does not leave it completely up to us. He works to bring it about in our lives.

But the Spirit produces love, joy, peace, patience, kindness, goodness, faithfulness, humility, and self-control. There is no law against such things as these (Gal. 5:22-23, GNB).

*

35

HOW LONG does it take to teach a Sunday School lesson?
Obviously, thirty minutes or so, depending upon the class situation with which you are familiar.

Actually, it depends.

It depends upon how much time it takes the teacher to prepare to teach the material *plus* how much time it takes to present it.

Many of our opportunities are like icebergs; most of the time they require is beneath the surface. Whether it's being an officer in the parent-teacher organization or chairing a committee, there's always more to the job than meets the eye.

Serenity is thinking through your opportunities before they become obligations. It is taking a hard look at your current commitments before coming to a conclusion. It is deciding what's important and making adjustments. Sometimes it is "faithing it" that we will have God's help in finding the needed time and energy to accomplish what we set out to do.

Sometimes it is just doing the best we can under the circumstances. For, so often, commitments are made far in advance, and in the meanwhile situations arise that change our priorities and obligations, situations we could neither predict nor avoid.

There is peace in knowing that God understands and the Holy Spirit's power is available to see us through.

*

"WHAT A hurry everyone is in over here!" exclaimed a German tourist when asked to comment on American life.

Rush, rush, rush does seem to be the name of the game for all too many people. Face-to-face communication is unheard of in some two-career marriages; couples communicate as they pass on the way to work.

"We never get to eat together as a family," say parents with teenagers who are busy with school, sports, and part-time jobs.

Even retirees are advising, "If you have anything you want to do, do it before you retire . . . you'll be too busy later on."

One of the memories I brought back from our vacation in England was of the many garden seats one finds in the parks and gardens of that lovely land. They were everywhere, inviting us to pause a while, to rest, to enjoy the beauty at leisure. "Don't rush through, please! Relax a moment, enjoy your surroundings," they seemed to be saying.

In Oban, Scotland, we found these classic seats along the esplanade, beckoning us a little further along the seashore. "Here, just ahead, is still another place to stop and rest."

We all need some resting places in our lives. Without them we may lose heart and wonder why. In them we find serenity and strength to go on.

The Lord is my Pace-setter,
I shall not rush;
He makes me stop and rest
for quiet intervals.
He provides me with images of stillness
which restore my serenity;
He leads me in ways of efficiency
through calmness of mind
and his guidance is my peace.
Even though I have a great many things
to accomplish each day,
I will not fret, for his presence is here.
His timelessness, his all importance
will keep me in balance.
He prepares refreshment and renewal
in the midst of my activity
By anointing my mind with his oils of tranquility.
My cup of joyous energy overflows.
Surely harmony and effectiveness
shall be the fruits of my hours
For I shall walk in the pace of my Lord
and dwell in his house forever.

*

NOT ONLY does one need places to sit for a while in a garden, but landscape designers insist that a fountain, a little waterfall, or a quiet pool of water is enhancing as well. Even a broad, low container brimming with water, they say, can bring a new dimension to your garden.

Beside a small lake on a campus one day I visited with a woman going through divorce. We talked, then sat quietly watching the wind-rippled surface that lay before us.

"It helps to take your troubles to moving water," my friend commented thoughtfully.

Maybe this is why the sea holds such an appeal for so many people. And why city planners include fountains and inland states develop vast reservoirs where their people can find respite from the daily grind.

And why folks go fishing!

Arthur Gordon, in his book *Touch of Wonder*, tells of a time when he had reached a standstill in his writing career. Finally he went to see an old doctor who gave him a prescription to be taken beside the sea, instructions about how to spend a single day.

He was to spend three hours listening very carefully, three hours reaching back into his memories, three hours reexamining his motives, and then he was to write his worries in the sand.

With a fragment of a shell Gordon says he wrote several words, one above the other, on the beach and then he walked away without looking back. He knew the tide was coming in.

To listen quietly for a while and then to reflect, to examine our motives and then to place our concerns before the Lord,

"Casting all your care upon him, for he careth for you" (1 Pet. 5:7)—what better way to handle our problems?

Therefore I say unto you, Take no thought for your life, what ye shall eat, or what ye shall drink, nor yet for your body, what ye shall put on. Is not the life more than meat, and the body than raiment?

Behold the fowls of the air: for they sow not, neither do they reap, nor gather into barns; yet your heavenly Father feedeth them. Are ye not much better than they?

Which of you by taking thought can add one cubit unto his stature?

And why take ye thought for raiment? Consider the lilies of the field, how they grow; they toil not, neither do they spin:

And yet I say unto you, That even Solomon in all his glory was not arrayed like one of these.

Wherefore, if God so clothe the grass of the field, which to-day is, and to-morrow is cast into the oven, shall he not much more clothe you, O ye of little faith?

Therefore take no thought, saying, What shall we eat? or, What shall we drink? or, Wherewithal shall we be clothed?

(For after all these things do the Gentiles seek:) for your heavenly Father knoweth that ye have need of all these things.

But seek ye first the kingdom of God, and his righteousness; and all these things shall be added unto you.

Take therefore no thought for the morrow: for the morrow shall take thought for the things of itself. Sufficient unto the day is the evil thereof (Matt. 6:25-34).

*

38

WE ALL need our retreats. Our homes are places to retreat to, away from the places of employment. A workplace can be a retreat from an unpleasant homelife. Church is a retreat from the demands life makes upon us for physical wants and needs.

Often we need momentary retreats from upsetting situations. A department store supervisor told me she goes to her desk and sits down, alone, for a while when she finds herself in an aggravating situation. "I know I shouldn't be on the floor when I'm upset, so rather than 'letting them have it,' I retreat to calm down, think the problem over, and pray."

Sometimes your only option may be a mental retreat to some peaceful scene from your past. A favorite of mine is the memory of going with Aunt Courtney down to the pasture to bring up the cows on a late afternoon in the hills of South Mississippi.

The smell of pines, unfamiliar to me then, still lingers, and I can still sense the touch of the cool green grass as I stretched out momentarily to look skyward through needled branches. The sound of the tinkling cowbells in the distance and a mental image of the long shadows alternating with lengths of waning sunlight still come back over the years at the thought of that magic moment.

Here, with this memory, I can be alone for a while. It is a place of privacy, a momentary retreat I can count on to give my mind and spirit a break.

There is a place of quiet rest,
Near to the heart of God;
A place where sin cannot molest,
Near to the heart of God.

There is a place of comfort sweet,
Near to the heart of God,
A place where we our Savior meet,
Near to the heart of God.

There is a place of full release,
Near to the heart of God;
A place where all is joy and peace,
Near to the heart of God.

 O Jesus, blest Redeemer,
 Sent from the heart of God,
 Hold us, who wait before thee,
 Near to the heart of God.
     — *C. B. McAfee*

*

39

IS THERE anything one can do to prepare for the loss of a loved one? Studying bereavement and the grief process I asked this practical question and, from what I learned from counselors and some who had suffered such loss, came up with five possibilities:

Create good memories.—Now is the time to begin living with our loved ones so we will have a maximum of joyous recollections and a minimum of regrets when they are gone. Certainly living to make life easier and more pleasant for those we love is a healthful, happy way to live—a way to serenity. But consider the serenity it produces after it is too late to participate in a particular relationship.

A chaplain advises living with as much openness as possible in the marriage relationship. Noting that guilt is a very real reaction following the death of a loved one, he said, "If a man and woman can hash out their differences and become reconciled to them as they arise, there need be no remorse. We need to deal with regrets while they are fresh, as they come up." A daily making-things-right-with-others leaves the conscience clear and the memory slate cleared of negative recollections.

Consider saying good-bye if there is time.—So often, I was told, the dying are deserted by their already grieving families, at a time when empathy, reliability, availability, and a reassurance of being loved is so desperately needed.

Develop meaningful interests and quality relationships beyond the family.—"When one's world is one's family, the loss is worse," a widow of some four months told me. "It's late to begin thinking about getting involved after your husband is gone. In a state of grief and loss, it is hard to suddenly decide to get involved."

Analyzing the sorrow of other widows, one wrote, "It seemed to me it was longest-lasting among those who had little or no creative or humanitarian outlet."

Feed your faith.—A woman whose husband became ill and was forced to take early retirement said she never really related to many of the truths she had heard in Sunday School and church until faced with this crisis. "Now," she said, "I understand." She had fed her faith and was the stronger for it.

A friend who lost a child and who was nursing her husband through a terminal illness declared, "God has given me resources upon which to draw." She has nurtured her faith in the God who cares and comforts.

Anticipate recovery.—The suffering that results from the loss of a loved one can seem interminable, but "the night is not forever." Recovery is not only possible; it is probable. Most people survive their grief and eventually begin, as Catherine Marshall put it, "to live again."

> *God of the storms and of the calms,*
> *we praise thee not only for the times of tranquility*
> *but also for the times of fury when winds twist trees*
> *and life jumbles our plans—*
> *for the world without storms*
> *and our lives without agony*
> *would bring us nothing to grow on.*
> *Make us glad for stormy weather. Amen.*
> — *Richard Wong*

*

40

"I'M SO discouraged I could . . ."

Cry? Quit? Die?

If you've said it, join the club!

Discouragement comes to everybody at one time or another. Someone has called it a tool of the devil, one he can use to get into lives where none of his other tools will work.

Discouragement is sure to come when we expect too much—of ourselves, of others, of life. But even when we are reasonably realistic, there come times in our lives when we lose heart, we lose our courage. We are discouraged.

It helps to keep moving. Quit thinking about that disagreeable task you've been putting off; go ahead and get started. Why think for three days about a job that'll take no more than fifteen minutes? Work has a way of helping us solve many problems. It can clear the mind dulled by laziness and inertia. It can lift spirits made dreary by inactivity and complaining.

Do some goal setting. Polish up your purposes. The sales manager of a big company employing women on a part-time basis says she finds her workers must be reminded periodically why they went to work in the first place. "They get their noses so close to their work they get nearsighted. So now and then I help them get their purposes out where they can see them again, and then together we shine them up so they go away with the urge to try a little harder."

Take three women in diverse circumstances. One is a professional. Another is a full-time homemaker. The third is a businesswoman handling a heavy workload at the office, as heavy an emotional load at home with a problem husband, and children who are practically her total responsibility. Each is living a triumphant life. No doubt they each have their moments of discouragement, but they do not appear to be living discouraged lives.

They have come to know and accept themselves. From somewhere deep within they have been able to determine what they can and cannot do, what they should and should not attempt. They realize the search for self-knowledge is a continuing process, for what might be true now may not be so later on. There is no conflict—it is merely the unfolding of the soul, as Gibran says, "like a lotus of countless petals."

They are day-at-a-timers, doing what needs to be done now and not getting too upset over what's left.

They don't have time to be constantly pulling up their roots to see if they are "growing." They are not trying to impress anyone, and they don't measure themselves by others.

They accept the "inalterables."

They look upon illness and other emergencies of life as divine interruptions. They find ways to live through each crisis with a measure of serenity, making the best of the situation.

They have made mistakes, of course. The professional thinks, *I should have done it this way. Next time. . . .* The housewife reasons, "If only I had started sooner. . . ." The businesswoman cries, "Glory hallelujah, I got experience!"

They can laugh at themselves.

They usually manage to get the rest they personally require for maximum performance.

They stand tall in the knowledge that they are God's creation, His handiwork, that He loves them, He even likes them. They are confident that He hears and answers prayer. With this kind of security they can stay on top of their circumstances.

But O my soul, don't be discouraged!
Don't be upset! Expect God to act!
For I know that I shall again have
plenty of reason to praise Him
for all that He will do!
He is my help!
He is my God! (Ps. 42:11, TLB).

*

41

GARDENING IN Denver, in many ways, is a lot like gardening anywhere else. You take one step at a time. You dig five-dollar holes for one-dollar plants. You water carefully, protect from the cold, and so on. But, as an authority on gardening in the Rockies advised, "Finally, you accept the dictates of our unusual mile-high climate gracefully, without losing your nerve."

Just as you have to adapt your recipes to the high altitude, you adapt your flower growing, also. But oh, it is worth it. I never saw more brilliant coloring. And how the blooms lasted!

There's a great deal of serenity to be found when we accept the unusual and adapt to it. And a great deal of misery otherwise!

I've been visiting with a woman whose husband has been tapped for a position entailing a move from Oklahoma to Virginia. "I've found peace about our plans," she says, "but ..." Things like the fact that he'll be traveling a great deal, that she has had to resign her job, that the house they've enjoyed so much must be sold and another found, that their children will be half a continent and more away, that she really thought they were settled.

But this woman has accepted the change and she will adapt.

... like Sarah, who probably never complained when Abraham said, "We're packing and moving tomorrow, dear, and I'm not sure where we're heading."

... and like Ruth, who, widowed and lonely, said in those famous words to her mother-in-law, "Whither thou goest, I will go; and where thou lodgest I will lodge; thy people shall be my people, and thy god my god" (Ruth 2:16).

... and like me, who, knowing all the time I'd go, wanted to shout no in the midst of a move to Denver. I didn't like leaving behind my accumulation of friends and memories and achievements in Missouri, but I looked up at the glistening Gateway Arch, St. Louis' proud symbol of America's westward movement, and saw in a vision women in sunbonnets, packing their things into covered wagons.

We women have always gone with our men. We have followed them to their new frontiers. We've struggled alongside them in clearing and carving out a new place under the sun. We accept the changes their careers offer, and given time, like plants recuperating from the shock of a transplant, we adapt.

For home is wherever we're together, and we dare them to try to leave us behind.

God, grant me
   the serenity to accept the things I cannot change,
   the courage to change the things I can change,
   and the wisdom to know the difference.

*

42

A WOMAN whose husband was an alcoholic never questioned whether or not she should continue to live with him. For years, though, she chafed at her deep disappointment and made excuses for her misery. In shame and self-pity she withdrew from all who could have made life worthwhile.

Then one day, with a sudden insight into what her reaction was doing to her children, she did an about-face. "I just decided I might as well accept my husband's problem and make the best of life in spite of it."

I'd like to report that the family received help and the husband was able to overcome his drinking problem, but I do not know. The woman's decision, however, transformed her home and may have saved her children's future, for their personalities blossomed with her change of attitude.

Looking at some of the circumstances of our lives, we can either reject them and become bitter—or accept them, roll up our sleeves, and do everything possible to better or make the best of the situation.

Paul Tournier, the Swiss physician and counselor, has written extensively of how very harmful any kind of rejection can be to a person and how very vital acceptance is. The way of acceptance is undoubtedly an answer to serenity, but it doesn't often happen overnight. Tournier observes that a long apprenticeship is necessary and that "all liberating growth takes time."

*

43

"SOMETIMES YOU have to dream a second-best dream!" writes a woman paralyzed from her waist up. "There are some situations where you may have to abandon hope for a complete reversal of disappointing circumstances, and other dreams must fill the void."

For a long time she dreamed of complete recovery. And then at last she realized that if not all first dreams are possible, another can take its place. A Denver resident, she had grown up in the shadow of the Rockies, and now she dreamed of being able to go up once again into the high country.

But her breathing capacity was scarcely sufficient to sustain her at lower elevations, and for years trips into the rarified atmosphere of the mountains were out of the question.

Then, with the help of a device which expanded her lung capacity, she was freed to realize her second-best dream. She wrote of the joy she experienced as she and her family drove west toward Loveland Pass on camping trips each summer. Though sometimes breathing became very painful for her and they had to hurry down, her second-best dream was realized.

The way of acceptance opens the spirit to "possible dreaming." When the door is shut upon some cherished hope, investigate the alternatives. Dream a possible dream. In it you may find serenity.

*

44

ONE MORNING in Denver we were having breakfast with our two-year-old grandson and his parents when he suddenly cried out, "Look, Mommy, there's a bug on my plate!"

"Oh, no, dear," his mother soothed. "That's just a speck of cinnamon."

"Cinnamon don't crawl," he insisted.

A closer look, and sure enough, Doug was right. There *was* an aphid on his plate. You see, before breakfast he had picked one of the huge Peace roses at our front doorstep and placed it in a glass right beside his plate. Thus the bug.

Remembering his mother's sincere apology, I am reminded of the serenity in those two little words, "I'm sorry."

Saying "I'm sorry" is almost a lost art these days. Employers are frequently extremely frustrated when employees goof and never once say, "I'm sorry." Customers with legitimate complaints seldom hear "I'm sorry" from companies responsible for faulty merchandise and the problems that result.

Parents and teachers hate to have to say, "I was wrong."

Husbands and wives can scarcely bring themselves to apologize to one another.

Children, compelled to say "I'm sorry" when they really don't mean it, remind us that the words said half-heartedly, with traces of bitterness and unresolved anger, can scarcely be called an apology.

Someone has said that making an apology takes some preparation, some shifting of the emotional gears. It can happen in a sudden insight, or it may take a sleepless night or a good sulk. You have to go through a process. Reconciliation has been described as an exercise in creativity.

But clearing the air is well worth the effort. Hurt feelings are soothed, contact, communication, and confidence restored, good relationships can be resumed. And life becomes serene once more.

Love's Prerogative

Love ever gives—
Forgives—outlives—
And ever stands
With open hands.
And while it lives,
It gives.
For this is Love's prerogative—
To give—and give—and give.
— John Oxenham

*

45

THE DRIVE up Mount Evans to Echo Lake was one of our favorites for giving our guests from the lowlands a view of Colorado's high country. Usually we took a picnic lunch to enjoy beside the lake. When our young nephews came we planned some fishing as well.

The excitement had been building since early morning, as the men got the fishing gear ready and we packed the car for the trip. Then came the drive up, with a stop at a lookout for hot chocolate and doughnuts. At last there it was—Echo Lake shining in the sun, just waiting to be fished.

But first the picnic. Eight-year-old Scott was asked to offer thanks. "And, Lord," he prayed earnestly, "help us be satisfied with our catch!"

Content with our catch—what an achievement! A basic contentment with who we are, how we look, what life has handed us, and what we have chosen makes for serenity. A popular magazine describes such an attitude as "living rich."

I like the story of an old woman who was haunted by the vague idea of a mysterious contentment with which other people were gifted but which she thought she had been denied. She made life utterly miserable for herself and everyone around her.

After many years of turbulent living, one day she did an about-face. She began to smile, to be pleasant. When someone finally got up the courage to ask what had brought about the drastic change, she said, "I don't know. All my life I've been a-strainin' and a-strugglin' to have a contented mind like other folks. But finally I decided I'd just settle down and be contented without one."

Let your conversation be without covetousness; and be content with such things as ye have: for he hath said, I will never leave thee, nor forsake thee. So that we may boldly say, The Lord is my helper, and I will not fear what man shall do unto me (Heb. 13:5-6).

*

46

DURING ONE of our most hectic years my husband and I took what we call our "canyon vacation." Heading west from Denver, we touched down at Oak Creek Canyon, Canyon de Chelly, Grand Canyon, and Bryce Canyon. It was at Canyon de Chelly where we came upon a primitive scene which, if moments had titles, I would call "Serenity."

We turned into an overlook beside the canyon late in the afternoon and slipped out of our car to get our first glimpse of this magnificent depth we would explore by jeep the next day.

As we stood silently looking downward, awed by its vastness, we heard a tiny sound, a faint tinkling. Then, our eyes adjusting to the distances, we saw a Navajo woman, a long stick in her hand, a dog playing close by. In a few minutes we found her sheep—the sound was coming from the lead goat's bell. In her long, colorful skirt our shepherdess seemed to float toward them, working slowly, now and then bending low to pick a few berries, we assumed.

Suddenly we heard other sounds, and a male Indian on horseback rounded the foot of the cliff to our right and turned back again, evidently enjoying a little gallop at the end of a day in his field.

How long we stood there I do not know, murmuring now and then about what we saw, contemplating privately what life must be like for these two.

Weary from the strain of recent events, I envied the tranquillity they obviously enjoyed, removed as they were from the hustle of life as we knew it in the city. This woman did not have the sounds of news and weather and insistent commercials to disturb her contentment. I thought, *what a relief it must be to be spared the pressure of too many daily choices.*

I admired the way she approached her task at day's end—unhurried and relaxed. She apparently had plenty of time to do what needed to be done toward the end of her day. I imagined her enjoyment of life as she found it.

Darkness comes early in a canyon, and it occurred to me that in a little while this woman would be able to turn to her husband with neither spent emotions nor jagged nerves marring their relationship.

Reflecting on this primitive scene, I've often wondered whether knowledge is always liberating . . . and whether too few choices are always worse than too many . . . if the presence of people assures contentment, and the acquiring of things freedom.

Anne Morrow Lindbergh found the serenity of simplicity beside the sea. I found it looking deep into an Arizona canyon.

Simplicity, the absence of complexity, is a continual challenge to most of us. In *Celebration of Discipline—The Path to Spiritual Growth* Richard Foster writes, "The spiritual discipline of simplicity is not a lost dream but a recurring vision throughout history. It can be recaptured today. It must be."

*

47

GOD, THOU ART LOVE

If I forget,
Yet God remembers! If these hands of mine
Cease from their clinging, yet the hands divine
Hold me so firmly that I cannot fall;
And if sometimes I am too tired to call
For Him to help me, then He reads the prayer
Unspoken in my heart, and lifts my care.

I dare not fear, since certainly I know
That I am in God's keeping, shielded so
From all that else would harm, and in the hour
Of stern temptation strengthened by His power;
I tread no path in life to Him unknown;
I lift no burden, bear no pain, alone:
My soul a calm, sure hiding-place has found:
The everlasting arms my life surround.

God, Thou art love! I build my faith on that.
I know Thee who has kept my path, and made
Light for me in the darkness, tempering sorrow
So that it reached me like a solemn joy;
It were too strange that I should doubt Thy love.
— Robert Browning

*

Part 3

Live Creatively

*See your creative potential,
the gift of a loving God*

48

IN OUR home there hangs a print of the painting *Madonna of the Prairie,* the original of which I saw on display at the Cowboy Hall of Fame in Oklahoma City. It pictures a young woman moving west, her halo the half-circle of the covered wagon on which she rides.

I cannot fully describe the look in her eyes; it is so poignant I could not bear to leave it hanging over my desk where I'd see it constantly.

Is she with child . . . is her child asleep there behind her in the wagon, and the look that of a mother concerned for his future . . . or has she left him in a little grave alongside the trail a week ago? I wonder . . .

Along with her most cherished possessions packed away in the wagon she must have the root of a yellow rose—her mother had got it from *her* mother, you know. Wrapped in damp rags, already it is beginning to sprout in the dark warmth of the covered wagon.

My madonna reminds me of the creativity of our pioneers to the West.

They set their goals and forged ahead to reach them.

They adapted.

They substituted.

They managed.

They combined time, energy, and ideas to build their homes, do their planting, raise their barns, and quilt.

They looked after one another in sickness and trouble.

They started schools and churches.

We are indebted to their creativity.

And I am sometimes ashamed at my laziness and lack of creativity in:

identifying my problems,
  setting goals and forging ahead,
    adapting,
      substituting,
        managing—
in making the most of my God-given potential for the better-
ment of family and mankind.

*Eternal God, keep me a lover of the old
and yet an explorer of the new. Keep me in the love of old songs,
old values, and old friends. Yet lead me to love the shock of a
new idea, a new day,
and a new chance to be what I truly ought to be. Amen.*
— *Richard Wong*

*

49

SHE WAS a Methodist minister's wife, and that meant a lifetime of moving about, living in houses owned and furnished by church members, building her life around her husband's commitment and call.

It took resourcefulness to make ends meet . . .

insight to understand the ways of some members of the congregation . . .

tact to get along with them . . .

and often a sense of humor to survive.

The thing her grandchildren remember about her is her love for gardening. For everywhere she went, she planted shrubs and flowers. Always she carried seeds and roots from one location to another, and in each place she found people glad to share their garden treasures.

All across the Midwest, they say, are little spots of beauty created by their beloved grandmother.

These were the gardens of her life, places of self-expression and fulfillment, where her holy awe at the miracle of growth and her gratitude for beauty flowed upward to God like a fountain. Here in her gardens she found renewed courage for daily dilemmas and it was here where solutions to her problems surfaced.

We all need a place somewhere in our lives to clear our minds, to express ourselves, and to regroup from time to time—if we are to live creatively.

. . . *A garden is a grand teacher. It teaches patience and careful watchfulness; it teaches industry and thrift; above all, it teaches entire trust. "Paul planteth and Apollos watereth, but God giveth the increase." The good gardener knows with absolute certainty that if he does his part, if he gives the labour, the love, and every aid that his knowledge of his craft, experience of the conditions of his place, and exercise of his personal wit can work together to suggest, that so surely as he does this diligently and faithfully, so surely will God give the increase. Then with the honestly-earned success comes the consciousness of encouragement to renewed effort, and, as it were, an echo of the gracious words, "Well done, good and faithful servant."*

— *Gertrude Jekyll*

*

50

THE SCHOOL where I worked had sent a number of its employees to a seminar on creativity, and the opening activity was proof enough that my creative powers left something to be desired. Some conferees had lists twice as long as mine.

The idea of applying imagination to everyday living fascinated me, however. Experiments, we were told, indicated that animals which have been caged for a long time will continue to pace in the same patterns even when given more freedom. I took away a little card depicting a lion in a cage, a reminder to "break the small cage habit."

Tiring of the uncertainties and rootlessness of substitute teaching, I had taken a job as receptionist and secretary to a school principal. And I was bored. I had already made a few changes in my small office and I saw little possibility for further change. A different route to work—maybe.

Getting ready to type the daily bulletin the next morning, an idea hit. I'd change my margin stops! I guess I'd typed a hundred of those bulletins, all in the same format. I'd always done it that way!

It was amazing what a lift I received from doing that one little task just a little differently. I was determined to break the small-cage habit.

Before long, in answer to specific prayer for a more challenging position, I found myself in a job which unleashed creative powers I did not dream existed.

Since then, when I realize I've fallen into a rut of routine I know it's time to change my margin stops. A rut, you know, is a grave with both ends knocked out!

In the rut of routine? It's time to change your margin stops. Rearrange your schedule, take time out for fun, read something different, try a new recipe, get some new place mats, make a new acquaintance, add something new to your wardrobe—change can give a new zest to life.

*

51

EXCEPT WITH reference to God, I do not find the word *create* or any of its derivatives in the King James Version of the Bible. In the truest sense of the word, only God creates. The power of intelligent combination, someone has said, is the nearest thing we can know to the mighty force of creation.

Yet we find superb examples of persons who were creative in the use of their God-given gifts, resources, and energy.

None stands out more than the virtuous woman described in Proverbs 31.

Here was a woman who was into real estate. She developed a vineyard. She ran a little cottage textile industry.

Besides all this, she saw to the endless details of a home—shopping, cooking, sewing, decorating.

She kept herself physically fit and attractively dressed.

She was spiritually perceptive.

A kind woman, she was benevolent to the poor, often going to them, not waiting for them to come to her.

She was a good wife and mother. Her husband boasted, "She's the greatest!"

She had great reverence for God.

Few women today have servant girls, as this woman did, to help with the work of the home. Yet never have there been so many ways to get housework done so easily and effectively. Still homemaking calls for creativity, and we are continually on the lookout for better ways.

We simplify . . .
   rearrange . . .
      eliminate . . .
         organize . . .
            devise . . .
               designate. . . .

With communication, creativity, and cooperation, home can be a happier place for everyone in the family.

Charm is deceptive
and beauty disappears,
but a woman who honors the Lord should be praised.
Give her credit for all she does.
She deserves the respect of everyone (Prov. 31:30-31, GNB).

*

52

WHERE WOULD you find a more creative person than the mother of Moses? She bore a son, "a goodly child," during that terrible time when, by decree of Pharaoh, every newborn Hebrew male was to be thrown into the Nile.

For three months she managed to hide the child. She must have prayed constantly, as only a mother can, for a way to save her little one. Then, when time was running out, she used her ingenuity to protect him.

Taking a basket of reeds which she may have woven herself, she covered it with tar to make it watertight. Enfolding the baby in her arms as she took him to her breast for what she knew might be the last time, she then placed him in the basket. Slipping down to the edge of the river, she set it among the tall grasses near the place where the king's daughter came to bathe.

The baby's mother then stationed his sister, Miriam, at a little distance to watch what would happen. Counting on the power of the maternal instinct, she must have instructed Miriam carefully about what to do when the child was discovered.

Sure enough, the unusual basket caught the eye of Pharaoh's daughter and she sent a maid for it. As she opened it up, there she found this beautiful little baby and he was crying. (Dr. R. G. Lee, the famous preacher from Memphis, Tennessee, said about that time an angel from God pinched him.)

"The little thing is hungry," the princess probably murmured to her maid. And, as the story goes on in Exodus 2, "she had compassion on him" (v. 6).

Enter Miriam, enthusiastically offering to go and find a Hebrew nurse. And so it was that the child who was to become one of the greatest leaders of all time was rescued, returned to his mother for nursing through infanthood, adopted by a princess, and brought up as royalty.

God had a plan for His people, and He inspired a caring mother to be creative in helping to fulfill that plan.

*

53

WHAT DO you do when your children consider themselves too old for a "baby-sitter"? At some point, you begin to leave them by themselves, of course. But what about in the meanwhile?

One mother with twin sons in third grade solved the problem with a word. She hired a "supervisor"!

With creativity, she solved two problems at once. Not only were the twins open to having a supervisor; the young man she employed maintained his dignity, too. He might have turned down a baby-sitting job!

The question mark is a tool of the trade for creative persons and it certainly comes in handy for parents. "How can I get Johnny to eat?" "What can I do to get Susie to practice piano regularly?" "What do you do to get your kids settled down at night?" "How do you punish a grounded teenager who's lost her telephone privileges?"

Anticipating,
   thinking through,
      considering alternatives,
         rearranging,
            rewarding, and asking such questions as "How or what else?" "What if . . .?" and "Why not . . .?" may produce the very solution you're searching for.

Creative parenting is an exciting challenge. It takes time and thought and effort. The advantages of team creativity are never more obvious than when two parents team up to think up ways of bringing up a child "in the way he should go." The rewards can be priceless.

Much of the glory of human life comes as we are conscious partners in creation.

— D. Elton Trueblood

*

THE PARENTS' CREED

I believe that my children are a gift of God—the hope of a new tomorrow.

I believe that immeasurable possibilities lie slumbering in each son and daughter.

I believe that God has planned a perfect plan for their future, and that His love shall always surround them; and so

I believe that they shall grow up!—first creeping, then toddling, then standing, stretching skyward for a decade and a half—until they reach full stature—a man and a woman!

I believe that they can and will be molded and shaped between infancy and adulthood—as a tree is shaped by the gardener, and the clay vessel in the potter's hand, or the shoreline of the sea under the watery hand of the mighty waves; by home and church; by school and street, through sights and sounds and the touch of my hand on their hand and Christ's spirit on their heart! So,

I believe that they shall mature as only people can—through laughter and tears, through trial and error, by reward and punishment, through affection and discipline, until they stretch their wings and leave their nest to fly!

O God—I believe in my children. Help me so live that they may always believe in me—and so in Thee.

— Robert H. Schuller

*

NEVER UNDERESTIMATE the potential of a person with an idea and the faith to see it through. Take the four men of Capernaum who brought their paralyzed friend, "one sick of the palsy," to Jesus.

One of them initiated the action: he was the man with the idea. He saw Jesus as the solution to his friend's problem.

Knowing he could not get the job done alone, he enlisted adequate help. He got the group together at a certain time, a certain place.

Taking the corners of the lame man's mat, the four men carried their friend through the streets to the house where Jesus was preaching to a crowd.

Mark 2:1-12 tells us that there they encountered a big hindrance to their plan—there was no way they could get through to Jesus.

So, typical of creative people, they made a way. "Hey, I know what we can do," one may have said. "Let's take him up onto the roof and get him in that way."

Imagine their difficulty in climbing those outside steps to the roof carrying the paralyzed man. One may have run to get some rope, for after making a large opening in the roof they managed to let their friend down carefully, right at the feet of Jesus.

And seeing the faith of these men, Jesus said to the handicapped man, "Son, thy sins be forgiven thee. . . . Arise, and take up thy bed, and go thy way."

Someone with an idea, with initiative, enlisting the cooperation of others, determined not to be stopped by hindrances, refusing to be discouraged, and using imagination to make a way when there is none, can bring about a miracle.

And the grandest outcome of all: like the crowd who watched

the healing of the man sick with palsy, observers are amazed and can glorify God as they exclaim, "We have never seen anything like this!" (v. 12, GNB).

O magnify the Lord with me, and let us exalt his name together (Ps. 34:3).

*

56

NEXT TIME you eat a peanut butter and jelly sandwich, thank God and a man who knew where to turn for creativity.

George Washington Carver, the black American educator and botanist, was distressed about the way Southern soil had been depleted by the growing of a single crop, cotton. Most black families planted a few peanuts because the children loved "goobers." They did not realize how the vines put nitrogen back into the soil, and they had no idea of the protein in the peanut.

But Carver had a notion that there was more to the peanut than met the eye, and, in faith, he asked his people to plant peanuts for a cash crop. He didn't quite know how these peanuts would be used, but he began to experiment.

He prayed, "Tell me, Great Creator, why did you make the peanut?"

In the early morning quiet, he seemed to hear a voice replying, "I have given you three laws—compatibility, temperature, and pressure. Observe these laws, and I will show you why I made the peanut."

Carver developed over three hundred products from the peanut and before he died in 1943 had discovered why God made a great many other things.

He is unique proof that God is faithful to His promise which we find in James 1:5-6a: "If any of you lack wisdom, let him ask of God, that giveth to all men liberally and upbraideth not; and it shall be given him. But let him ask in faith, nothing wavering."

*

57

THE MEADOW which lies just beyond our dining area is in bloom right now, a coverlet of yellow and white. The surrounding areas have been mowed once, but we always leave the meadow untouched at this stage. Walking there last Sunday afternoon we discovered drifts of blue flowers, also, an overlay of color not visible from a distance but gorgeous to look upon.

I am reminded of another Sunday afternoon when young parents strolled in a field near their apartment, the children, one in Daddy's arms, the others scarcely knee-high, now holding onto a mother's finger, then scampering ahead. It was an experience to remember, a day of discovery, as the family knelt to observe the loveliness of the tiny wild flowers of Texas.

One doesn't have to look so closely for much of the beauty our God has created. The magnificence of the mountains, the matchless scene of an uncluttered seashore, the rolling landscape around us demand attention.

Here and there men fence in beauty and keep it under lock and key, but by and large the beauties of God's world offer "Free admission." The price we pay is simply in terms of time and a desire to behold—and, of course, sometimes the time and effort of getting there.

My mother looked for and found beauty in the commonest things. She would grow ecstatic over an ordinary brown branch. What most folks call weeds came across beautiful to her. Arrangements of twisted vine, curved garlic stalks, and gnarled wood adorned her home. She blessed me with her eye for beauty.

My father showed me the sky. One of my strongest memories of a moment shared with him was a Christmas Eve when he took me outdoors to look at the stars. The heavens declared the glory of God that night, and thanks to my daddy, I experienced it.

I owe my parents a debt of gratitude for my awakened eye, yet still there is a world of beauty I fail to see.

On a scale of one to ten, how do you rate in terms of creative seeing? If your rating is low, walk with a friend or relative or a child and look through his/her eyes for a while.

Look for something lovely on your way to work today—a lawn, a brilliant bed of periwinkles, a stately tree.

Check your windows (I hope you have a wide window in your workplace). Which has the best view? Are you hiding beauty behind heavy drapes?

That blank wall there—could you add a beautiful print, a likeness of a bit of God's beautiful world?

Live creatively. Open your eyes. Help yourself to beauty.

My Neighbor's Roses

The roses red upon my neighbor's vine
Are owned by him, but they are also mine.
His was the cost, and his the labor, too,
But mine as well as his the joy, their loveliness to view.

They bloom for me and are for me as fair
As for the man who gives them all his care.
Thus I am rich, because a good man grew
A rose-clad vine for all his neighbor's view.

I know from this that others plant for me,
And what they own, my joy may also be.
So why be selfish, when so much that's fine
Is grown for you, upon your neighbor's vine.
— *Abraham L. Gruber*

*

58

WE TOOK the Flying Scotsman, the fast train from London to Edinburgh, for our trip to Scotland. It was a wonderful way to view mile upon mile of English countryside, all seemingly manicured to parklike perfection.

The sheep help keep it so. An "Adopt a Sheep" program gives citizens an opportunity to participate by paying for the cost of putting sheep in shabby and unkempt areas.

Back in the States an "Adopt a Pothole" plan for getting streets in better working condition has proved successful in at least one city.

When the "usual" won't work, consider other possibilities.

Here is just a glimpse of what living creatively is all about, according to Alex F. Osborn, author of *Applied Imagination:*

Creativity

    looks forward . . .

    foresees . . .

    supplies . . .

    completes . . .

      plans . . .

      invents . . .

      solves . . .

      advances . . .

        originates . . .

        hunts . . .

        changes . . .

        mixes . . .

The creative person, he writes, asks idea-spurring questions such as . . .

    How can we adapt?

    Could we modify? What about a new twist?

Should we magnify . . . add something . . . give it more time?

Or maybe minimize? Streamline? Omit?

Or possibly substitute? What about a totally different approach?

Rearrange? Change pace? Change schedule?

Juggle the elements? Change roles?

Combine? How about a blend?

Creative thinking applied to problems, large and small, can provide solutions. One evening in a prayer service a businessman described a problem he was having in his work. "I prayed about it," he said. "I asked God to solve it for me. And you know what He did? He threw it right back into my lap!"

That's how we grow—not by having everything done for us, but by having to think through, to make decisions, to act responsibly. God is a good and loving God to give us such powers and to insist upon our using them. It is for our good and to His glory.

*

59

ONE OF the most fascinating aspects of the infinite creativity of God is the fact that He not only made such a wonderful world, but that He provided us with the senses with which to enjoy it.

Not only did He form the lovely rose; He gave us eyes to see its beauty.

Not only did He add fragrance to our food; He gave us the sense of smell.

Not only did He make the luscious peach; He gave us the ability to taste its goodness.

Not only did He make the mockingbird sing; He gave us ears to hear its song.

Not only did He make the gentle breezes of a warm summer evening; He gave us the pleasure of feeling them.

Beauty and fragrance and sound and softness and good things to eat without our five senses would be such a waste.

With the psalmist let us glorify the Master Creator, "O Lord our Lord, how excellent is thy name in all the earth!" (Ps. 8:1,9).

God who touchest earth with beauty,
Make me lovely too;
With Thy Spirit recreate me,
Make my heart anew.

Like Thy springs and running waters,
Make me crystal pure;
Like Thy rocks of towering grandeur,
Make me strong and sure.

Like Thy shining waves in sunlight,
Make me glad and free;
Like the straightness of the pine trees,
Let me upright be.

Like the arching of the heavens,
Lift my thoughts above;
Turn my dreams to noble action,
Ministries of love.

God, who touchest earth with beauty,
Make me lovely too;
Keep me ever, by Thy Spirit,
Pure and strong and true.
— Mary S. Edgar

*

60

WHEN GOD made man, He must have planned for him to pray. Think of God walking in the Garden of Eden in the cool of the day. Imagine the serene companionship Adam and Eve enjoyed with Him in those days before their disobedience. They were communicating with God.

Jesus—the perfect, sinless Son of God—spent a great deal of time praying. He did not have to pray for forgiveness, but He felt the need to talk with His Father. Anyone in a helping vocation will tell you that helping people is draining, both emotionally and physically, and Jesus was no exception. He needed strength to carry out the Father's will; He needed the renewal that prayer can provide.

Jesus' habits of prayer have helped many Christians: He set aside ample time for prayer; He found a quiet place where He could be alone with His Father; and He prayed earnestly early in the day.

Most of the time I pray with pen in hand. Getting my thoughts into writing helps me express my deepest needs to God. My mind tends to wander when I am still, and writing my conversations with God helps me be more coherent. I pray more specifically since I started prayer writing. Once in a while I look back and discover that answers which might easily have escaped my notice have come like the silent snow of a winter night.

Days when I can scarcely get going I rely on the model prayer, commonly known as the Lord's Prayer. It provides an excellent outline to enlarge upon and personalize.

No two people pray alike, and you may laugh at the thought of writing your prayers. But the psalms are filled with written prayers, and so are Paul's letters. You can find them all through the Bible. I challenge you to try it sometime—write a prayer.

*

61

MISS MARY Steele was a retired schoolteacher who lived in the Home for Aged Baptists near Ironton, Missouri.

A tall, gaunt woman, I never saw her when she was not neatly dressed. And she was invariably pleasant.

Miss Mary was a woman of devotion. Even after more than half a century of Christian discipleship, she never tired of studying God's Word.

She had a remarkable talent for human relationships. Miss Mary had the qualities that made guests glad they had come to visit her.

She was a respected leader among the residents. She was always ready to counsel and comfort.

And not least of all, she affirmed and encouraged the staff members.

Measured by the definition of wisdom found in James 3:17, Miss Mary was a wise woman:

But the wisdom that comes from heaven
is first of all pure and full of quiet gentleness.
Then it is peace-loving and courteous.
It allows discussion
and is willing to yield to others;
it is full of mercy and good deeds.
It is wholehearted and straightforward
and sincere (TLB).

In summer time one never really knows how beautiful are the forms of the deciduous trees. It is only in winter, when they are bare of leaves, that one can fully enjoy their splendid structure and design, their admirable qualities of duly apportioned strength and grace of poise; and the way the spread of the many-branched head has its equivalent in the wide-reaching ground-grasp of the root . . . . Old apple trees are specially noticeable for their beauty in winter, when their extremely graceful shape, less visible when in loveliness of spring bloom or in rich bounty of autumn fruit, is seen to fullest advantage.

— *Gertrude Jekyll*

*

62

SOME OF the greatest creativity in our time has come because of our heightened awareness of the handicapped among
us. A columnist in the *Daily Oklahoman* recently gave space to
someone who wanted to share how bathtubs can be rigged for
use by arthritics. A regular weekly feature in the paper is
devoted entirely to hints for the handicapped. Sears, Roebuck
and other companies have specialized catalogs describing all
manner of devices and clothing for persons with disabilities.

An ingenious invention called LIFELINE(R) in use in all fifty
states and Canada now makes it possible for a disabled person
or one with medical problems to live independently. A small
"help button" worn around the neck can be pressed to call for
help, or if the person becomes inactive an automatic timer
alerts the hospital.

In California an interior designer teaching future building
designers requires each student to spend three hours shopping
from a wheelchair and another three wearing glasses smeared
with vaseline (to simulate cataracts). She says she can explain
the predicament of the frail elderly and the handicapped, but
it's better to let the students experience the problems themselves. On a different level a bank includes similar training for
its tellers, even having them put popcorn in their shoes and
take a turn standing in line.

That's creativity on the job.

Creative persons are not only interested in improving the
quality of life for themselves but for others, as well. And usually they are glad to share what they discover.

*

63

NOWHERE IS God's creativity more evident than in the way He answers prayer.

Our family continues to marvel at the creative way God met our need for a home in our retirement years. We were late starters in ministry, with my husband getting his college and seminary education after we married. During our years of working with churches we lived in church-owned housing.

For many years we were a single-income family with little or no money to invest for our future needs. Later, I went to work outside the home, and we poured all our resources into education for our daughters.

So when we found ourselves faced with the need of a home after retirement, we scarcely knew where to turn. Costs were up, interest rates soaring. The small inheritance from Carl's mother would help but not nearly enough.

At last, at the insistence of our daughter Nancy and her husband, we got serious about the matter and began to pray earnestly for guidance. I guess we had secretly hoped someone would just up and give us a place to live.

No one did, but God used our children to answer our prayer. Nancy and Jim had moved from Missouri to settle in Oklahoma. Accumulated funds in their teachers' retirement accounts had to be invested and they were considering real estate. Jim, a math teacher, had always wanted to try his hand at building.

"Mom and Dad," they approached us, "let's combine our resources and build a house. It will be yours as long as you wish to live in it."

Granted, it was one big project! Hard work from start to finish. Under Jim's and Nancy's leadership we nailed and sanded and stained and painted for months. But when the house was completed, we stood back and admired our handiwork, knowing how God must have felt on the sixth day of creation—that it was good.

It shouldn't have surprised us, for if the Lord could feed five thousand with a lad's little lunch, surely He can see that two of his longtime servants will not be left out in the cold.

But we continue to marvel at God's creativity. We bring to Him problems which defy solution. And He taps people and resources we would never have dreamed of to take care of the situation.

Now unto him that is able to do exceeding abundantly above all that we ask or think, according to the power that worketh in us, Unto him be glory in the church by Christ Jesus throughout all ages, world without end. Amen (Eph. 3:20-21).

*

64

THE PINK surprise lilies surprised us again by springing up a couple of weeks ago, a glorious bouquet set upon the mat of green crushed velvet lawn south of the house. The bulbs were hard, dry things when we planted them several years ago. A gift, they were unmarked and we didn't know what to expect. In spring, we learned, their foliage appears, then disappears completely. Then, as we go on about the business of summer, forgetting them completely, the long-stemmed blossoms show up unexpectedly in August.

These lilies are perennial reminders of how God answers prayer. So often splendid surprises come, long after we have forgotten our vague petition.

When one of our grandchildren lay critically ill in a St. Louis hospital, I was surprised by God's creativity in answering prayer. Of course, I prayed most diligently for our child, but then I prayed, too, for her parents. My prayer went something like this, "And, Lord, somehow please strengthen them during the painful hours of waiting."

When it looked as though little Pam would not survive, I stood beside her parents at the hospital and watched God answer prayer. The miracle of healing began to take place in a beautiful way.

And God didn't overlook my prayer for the parents, either. A young medical student decided to spend his Christmas holidays as a volunteer assistant to the physician who was caring for Pam. He took a special interest in the little patient, but best of all he proved to be a good companion and reassuring friend to the young parents.

Don't say these things just happen. God answers prayer

. . . yet we are sometimes surprised by the unusual ways by which He responds to our requests.

*

65

AFTER WEEKS of unusually hot, dry weather, at last there's relief. The past two weeks have been delightfully cool, and this Labor Day weekend has brought a long, slow rain.

Our fall garden has been planted. The greens are up and growing, and squash and beans are sprouting. It should be a good year for this, our first try at fall gardening.

The rain has freshened the shrubs and trees. The rose-colored zinnias are aglow, and the cypress vine with its tiny red blooms is a soft mass of green reaching all the way to the top of the greenhouse. Beyond the greenhouse on the other side, the asparagus bed vies for equal time, the delicate ferns reaching shoulder height and higher.

The showers refresh my spirit, too. The coolness they bring makes me want to get on with the housecleaning and yard work I've been putting off.

They remind me of the renewal that comes when we seek God's forgiveness for our sins. There's a cleansing that takes place when we take our wrongdoings to the Lord and leave them there. And, along with the cleansing, our lives seem to soak up more of God's love, revitalizing us for the days that lie ahead.

Thou visitest the earth, and waterest it:
thou greatly enrichest it with the river of God,
which is full of water:
thou preparest them corn,
when thou hast so provided for it.
Thou waterest the ridges thereof abundantly:
thou settlest the furrows thereof:
thou makest it soft with showers:
thou blessest the springing thereof.
Thou crownest the year with thy goodness;
and thy paths drop fatness.
They drop upon the pastures of the wilderness:
and the little hills rejoice on every side.
The pastures are clothed with flocks;
the valleys also are covered over with corn;
they shout for joy, they also sing (Ps. 65:9-13).

*

66

MY FRIEND looked absolutely wonderful, a picture of health and well-being. "How was your summer?" I asked.

The face of this school counselor, a single parent, shone as she described the business she and her teenage son had developed. It all started with her mother's friend inquiring about good yard help. To get going, they borrowed tools from her uncle.

It became a lawn-care enterprise, a mother-son partnership, with all sorts of fringe benefits in addition to income. Mother was teaching son about being reliable, about attention to detail, about customer relations, about private enterprise.

"We each receive ten dollars an hour for weeding," she marveled. "Just for pulling weeds!"

I walked away, inspired by the resourcefulness of one single parent, determined to prepare her son for the realities of life.

And I went back to my weeding thinking, "Why, every hour I do this I'm saving ten dollars. This work has value. I never thought of it that way before!"

It depends on how you look at things!

*

67

I NEED to wash windows! Last spring I decided I'd try to be creative about this recurring task.

First, I needed to get the "big picture." Do I indeed need to do windows? Where does washing windows fit into my life?

Then I remembered—the view! It had been love at first sight. I had insisted upon wide windows, lots of glass, so all could enjoy this pastoral setting.

Though most are low windows, in the past I've used a stepladder to reach the higher sections. Wasn't there a better way? Why not that picnic bench over there? (I got it for a dollar at a garage sale.) It was perfect. I could do *two* windows without moving the bench.

Usually the cleanup, after the windows were done, was a chore. Paper towels everywhere. Why not a bucket big enough to hold cleaner, paper, and other supplies? Of course, why hadn't I thought of that before?

Now I'm reminding myself that with a little creativity window washing is a snap.

Yes, I do windows.

The question now is, When do I start?

*

68

THE FIRST time I ever planted tulips, I rushed home from work, excited over my venture into gardening. Reading the instructions carefully, my husband and I planted each bulb the exact depth recommended.

As we dug away, enjoying the crisp fall afternoon, our next-door neighbor leaned over the fence to superintend.

"I don't want to discourage you folks," he said, shaking his head, "but sometimes bulbs like that rot in the ground during the winter . . . . A lot of times you'll see squirrels digging them up and carrying them away . . . . And then there are the gophers, they burrow in and eat them."

He makes me tired, I thought, and kept right on digging. After all, the instructions on the package said, "Just put 'em in the ground and walk away whistling."

Some call it hope. Throughout the Bible we find the word *hope*—"[love] hopeth all things"; "hope maketh not ashamed"; "rejoicing [in] hope"; and "Christ [Jesus], . . . the hope of glory." The apostle Paul placed hope right along with faith and love: "And now abideth faith, hope, [love] these three." Hope has been called the blossom of faith.

Hope is indispensable to creativity and accomplishment. A famous Western artist told me, "As I complete a painting, something seems to take over and give it the finishing touches. I sign it with a flourish, and it is done." He walks away whistling.

A metal sculptor in Santa Fe, asked which of his magnificent pieces he considered his masterpiece, replied, "My next one!" That's hope.

We writers drop a manuscript into the mail and walk away

whistling. After all, the best of a book, said O. W. Holmes, is not the thought which it contains, but the thought which it suggests. "Many ideas grow better when transplanted into another mind than in the one where they sprung up." Whatever our task, whether gardening, homemaking, parenting, a job in the marketplace or whatever, when we've followed instructions and given it our best, we should be able to "walk away whistling."

On an autumn day I shared my "Walk away whistling!" experience with a group of writers and artists and gave each of them a tulip bulb as a memento. The following spring I received this note and poem:

"Thank you for our Easter tulip. I had planted it by the fence in front of my kitchen window—and forgotten it. Then suddenly—

Our Easter Tulip:
The Miracle Cup

Gnarled, drained, irrevocably dead,
We buried you in our soil so hard and cold,
Abandoning you to snow and rain overhead,
Not dreaming the miracle soon to unfold.
Christ's blood-red cup you rise to hold
Is a generous offering to our world from God,
Overcoming, transfiguring our errant sod.
—Rosemary Gibson

How good God is to make us creatures of hope . . . and to give us tulips as symbols of hope. Just put 'em in the ground and walk away whistling!

Hyacinths to Feed the Soul

If of thy mortal goods thou art bereft,
And from thy slender store two loaves alone to thee are left,
Sell one, and with the dole
Buy hyacinths to feed thy soul.

— Gulistan of Moslih Eddin Saadi

*

69

I thank Thee, Lord, for life:
For Thou hast made and dowered me
With gifts of hearing, sight and speech,
With mind alert, and will that's free;
Guard all from harm, I Thee beseech.

I thank Thee, Lord, for health:
For day by day the joy of life
Runs through my veins with keen delight,
And I am glad amid the strife;
Keep my thoughts pure, guide me aright.

I thank Thee, Lord, for strength:
For as years pass, a fuller sense
Of power to dare and do is mine;
In active limb and muscle tense
I feel my strength: let it be Thine.

I thank Thee, Lord, for home:
Dear gift of Thine, where constant thought
Of parents' love forestalls my need;
Where care for others' weal is taught
And I am saved from self and greed.

I thank Thee, Lord, for hope:
What yet shall be I may not know;
The unseen days will changes bring,
And I shall have my song to sing.

— J. Williams Butcher

*

Part 4

Bring Your Caring Touch to Life

"Beloved, if God so loved us,
we ought also to love one another"
(1 John 4:11).

70

WE'VE BEEN out planting berry vines, a gift of the woman who lives beside the post office.

We got acquainted over her huge evergreen vine, the likes of which I've not seen elsewhere. As a newcomer to town, I asked the postmaster if he knew what kind of vine it was. He looked at me oddly, as if to say, "Lady, I've been asked a lot of questions in the course of my career, but this one tops them all!"

When I finally met the owner of the vine, she said she didn't know the variety; someone had brought her a start from another part of the state, and would I like a start?

Since then, she and I have had a give-and-take kind of friendship, and the berry vines were our latest acquisition.

Nowhere will you find more generosity than among people who love plants. I look about my yard this morning and find irises, daisies, peonies, honeysuckle, nandinas, altheas, and currants—all from the yards of plant-loving acquaintances.

In a few years the berry vines will begin to bear. Soon the cannas from Bertie and the yucca from the Thompsons will begin to sprout.

These gifts remind me that I am loved.

And I shall pass them on.

*

71

FOR YEARS I thought "ministry" was something my husband, the pastor, did. The activities I was involved in at the church I thought of as "church work." The inevitable responsibilities of a minister's wife—answering phone and doorbell and listening to troubled people—I considered all "a part of the job."

If only I had known the true meaning of "ministry," how much happier a Christian I would have been!

Dr. Elton Trueblood, the Quaker philosopher, helped me most of all as he persistently wrote that "Every Christian is a minister." I believe it was he who wrote that the words "to minister" are among the loveliest in the Christian vocabulary.

I knew, of course, that Jesus said He came not to be ministered unto, but to minister and to give His life a ransom for many.

But not until I took a job outside my home did it really dawn upon me that life does not really consist in the abundance of things one does "for the church" but in how one lives in the daily grind of life.

In the working world plenty of opportunities for ministry surfaced. There was the Cuban refugee whose desk was just outside my door. There were people who came from cultured, upper middle-class backgrounds, and a few who had been economically deprived. Among them were the cynical, the disillusioned, the immoral. It was a veritable mission field.

"Ministry," I learned, looking the word up in the dictionary, is not necessarily a "Christian" word—it means "meeting the needs of another." Of course, for the Christian it takes on deeper meaning as we realize that we are "[God's] workmanship, created in Christ Jesus unto good works, which God hath before ordained that we should walk in them" (Eph. 2:10).

Mother Teresa calls it doing "something beautiful for God."

> *If I can stop one Heart from breaking*
> *I shall not live in vain*
> *If I can ease one Life the Aching*
> *Or cool one Pain,*
> *Or help one fainting robin*
> *Unto his Nest again,*
> *I shall not live in Vain.*
> — *Emily Dickinson*

*

72

"MINISTRY" IS much more than "church work." A woman was bemoaning the fact she could no longer "do anything for the Lord." You see, after she was widowed she opened a child-care center in our small town where she kept a number of children from low-income families. She could no longer do the usual—attend women's daytime meetings and serve on committees as she had in the past.

Yet I have known her to care for children all night when parents didn't pick up their children, to take in a woman and two children who had nowhere else to go, then enlist community assistance in getting them settled in a house, to weep as she spoke of children who had never attended Sunday School. Talk about ministry—she may have been doing more than anyone else in town!

Meeting another's need may not always be a pleasant experience, yet there's joy when you come to the end of a day and realize, "Hey, I ministered to someone today!"

The circle of our lives includes many relationships—spouse, children, extended family, work associates and patrons, church family, neighbors, community acquaintances, people of other places and nations.

There are a world of things you can do for God without ever being elected, and often without going out of your way. "Think ministry"—it was our Lord's way of life. Make it yours, too. Bring your caring touch to life.

Joyful, joyful, we adore Thee,
God of glory, Lord of love,
Hearts unfold like flow'rs before thee,
Op'ning to the sun above.
Melt the clouds of sin and sadness;
Drive the dark of doubt away;
Giver of immortal gladness,
Fill us with the light of day!

All thy works with joy surround thee,
Earth and heav'n reflect thy rays,
Stars and angels sing around thee,
Center of unbroken praise.
Field and forest, vale and mountain,
Flow'ry meadow, flashing sea,
Singing bird and flowing fountain,
Call us to rejoice in thee.

Thou art giving and forgiving,
Ever blessing, ever blest,
Wellspring of the joy of living,
Ocean depth of happy rest!
Thou our Father, Christ our Brother—
All who live in love are thine;
Teach us how to love each other,
Lift us to the joy divine.
                              — Henry van Dyke

*

73

SOMEONE HAS told of a little boy, put to bed for the night, who became frightened during an electrical storm.

"Daddy, come here, I'm scared," he called.

"Oh, don't be afraid, son," his daddy replied. "God will take care of you."

"But, Daddy, right now I need somebody with skin on!"

People need people. Most have heard that God loves them. Many believe it to be true. Yet all of us need to know that some other human being cares about us.

A little caring may go a long way. It may make an indelible impression upon a life.

Several years ago my husband received a phone call from California. A man's voice said, "Brother Nelson, I just had to call to thank you for saving my life." The man (I'll call him Ben) was someone we'd ministered to some twenty-five years before, when he was a small child.

Ben and his brother came to our Sunday School, and Ben's brother had taken some money from a birthday bank in his Sunday School department. When confronted, he said he thought it wasn't wrong, so long as no one saw him do it.

Later, my husband noticed these children loitering around town after school, and he knew they were headed for trouble. Their mother, a single parent, worked in a neighboring town, so my husband brought them home one afternoon, planning to talk with her that evening about arranging regular after-school care.

We don't recall how many days they were with us after school, but for years, when we'd have porcupine meatballs and mashed potatoes for supper, we'd reminisce about how those boys ate! As time passed, we almost forgot them.

Now here was the younger of the two, a grown man, going to a great deal of trouble to locate us in order to say thank you. He had grown discouraged, disillusioned, and despondent, he said. One evening recently he had taken an overdose.

Just as he was passing out, Ben said my husband's face floated across his consciousness and he thought, *Brother Nelson cares about me. He cares what happens to me.*

Groping for the telephone, he called for help, and the paramedics who came to his rescue declared they arrived just in the nick of time.

It was no big thing we did, taking those boys into our home to play with our children for a few days. Simply put, one Christian man saw a need, enlisted his wife's help, and together we ministered to those children.

Ben's call continues to remind us that some of the seemingly insignificant things we do for others permanently shape lives.

There are as many ways to say "We care"
as there are persons in the Lord's church.

*

74

NO TWO people bring their caring touch to life in exactly the same way. Those who are best at "bake and take" have their specialties. One is famous for her pound cakes, another for her angel food, still another for her casseroles, and yet another for her lemon pies. A busy bank employee takes little baskets of packaged snacks.

Those who minister by listening *listen* uniquely. Comfort comes in a variety of shapes, textures, and colors.

God has given us unique personalities through which to express Christ-in-us to others. It is He who has gifted us for ministries in and through His church, and it is He who has granted us resources to use in bringing our caring touch to life.

Happy is the person who finds modes of ministry that seem "right" for him/her. Often we explore a number of possibilities before discovering the ministry or ministries for which we are best suited.

An artist who is also an expert in floral arranging writes to flower arrangers, "When we do find a medium that fits our needs—and use it—then into our lives comes fulfillment and a sense of peace." Even so, we will sense when we are ministering according to God's will for our lives.

James E. White, leading a conference on spiritual gifts, reminded me that we are gifted by God's own decision and by His grace: "We need to identify our gift, the special ability which the Holy Spirit, in accord with God's grace, gives every Christian to be used in ministry for the purpose of accomplishing the will of God within the body of Christ."

Many of us, he noted, get hooked into doing things we are not equipped to do. But as we identify our gift, we gain freedom to say no to our own ideas and others' invitations to become involved in various ministries that may not be quite right for us.

Knowing what our gift, or "medium," is, we are freed to operate within our own giftedness. Joy, fulfillment, and a sense of peace, rather than frustration, will be our reward.

The important thing is not so much *how* we care, as *that* we care some way, somehow.

> *God is accustomed to working*
> *through the partial, little accomplishments*
> *of fallible men and women.*

*

75

MAGNOLIA BLOSSOMS remind me that I am loved. And so do yellow roses.

On one of the saddest days of my life, a birthday, there was a knock at our back door and there I found a man from our church, a little Portuguese baker, bearing a lovely birthday cake for me. The yellow roses upon it seemed to say, "See how you are loved."

Tulips also remind me that I am loved. The queen-size quilt, each block in the tulip design made and signed by women of a church where my husband was interim pastor, carries its special message of love.

Likewise, I realize I am loved as I spread the fine linen tea cloth given me by our hostess and friend, Irene Russell of London—"to remind you of the tulips and daffodils you've enjoyed so much in England."

Some people seem to be gifted of God in the art of giving. Their gifts, small or large, have a way of saying, "See how you are loved."

It's the little personal touches, both tangible and intangible, that make life bearable at times.

A gardener brings his gift of potatoes and green beans to a feeble widow.

A deacon prunes her rose bushes.

Her neighbor replaces a light bulb.

The teenager next door carries out her trash.

A retired beautician manicures her nails and shampoos her hair.

A visitor brings news from her church and prays with her.

Each would likely dismiss what they've done with, "This is something I can do—no big thing."

Together, they offer a bouquet of kindness.

A simple, thoughtful deed may provide the incentive for hurting persons to carry on. A woman who received a call that several family members in a distant state had been killed in an accident described how a seemingly insignificant ministry moved her to action.

In the wake of the shock the husband of a co-worker at church, a quiet man, knocked on her door saying, "I've come to clean your shoes." And, as he proceeded to clean and polish the family's dirty shoes, she gathered strength to prepare for their flight to be with their loved ones.

Few of us have spectacular abilities and resources for caring. But what if all the caring in the world were left to those with exceptional gifts to share? Someone has said that the woods would be very silent if no birds sang but the best.

Ken Carter has worded a prayer for the Christian who wants to say, "See how you are loved":

"God, create for me an opportunity. Make me aware of it, for I want the world to see the difference that Jesus has made in my life."

> *Find out what God would have you do,*
> *and do that little well;*
> *For what is great and what is small,*
> *The Lord alone can tell.*

*

76

GOD HAS provided abundant resources for our use in ministering. Consider how time, money, special skills, the ability to relate to people, strong interests and hobbies that can provide a base for friendship, the ability to empathize, transportation, business or professional expertise and contacts, your home, your prayers might be used in bringing your caring touch to life.

And don't forget the value of life experiences as a resource for ministry.

Ernie and Gladys use their bouts with cancer as a basis for ministry to families. They've been there; they know whereof they speak and can offer encouragement, hope, and practical tips to ease the burden these families carry.

A nurse who at one time was severely depressed told me she receives frequent calls from physicians to go and minister to patients who are deeply depressed. She had attempted suicide, but she recuperated and went on to get her degree in nursing. She is living proof that there is life after depression.

I am impressed with the hope and help available in what I call "the literature of courage." The popularity of this type of reading material is evidence of the far-reaching ministry that writers perform as they share how they and others have coped with tragedy.

What you have learned in your struggle through a crisis of any kind—whether it's a new baby, the "terrible threes" or troubled teens, divorce, single parenting, retirement or job loss, or caring for an aging relative—can become your gift to others in a similar situation.

We all need someone who understands. We know that our Lord does, that He alone can enter what we feel and help us bear the burden of our pain, but it is a blessed thing to experience the caring touch of someone who has been there, too.

To tell what he has tried to do,
and how he has tried to think,
may be the most important service
one person can render to another.
As we all walk essentially the same path,
we stumble the less if our predecessors have left a few markers.
It is the duty of each person who has profited from some guidance to leave a few markers of his own.

— D. Elton Trueblood

*

77

I WAS on the verge of burnout as a Sunday School teacher when my young adult class began to think seriously about ministry. There were a great many older people in our church and the community, and there was no senior citizens' center to give direction and opportunity for socialization.

Church-sponsored clubs for mature adults were still uncommon at the time, so we cautiously explored the possibilities. The young adults were willing to do much of the legwork, but we knew the senior adults needed to be involved also. We secured church approval, laid our plans carefully, and announced the first meeting. We didn't know whether two or twenty would show up!

That ministry is now nearly ten years old and I understand it's still going strong. From our first timid offerings of quilting and macramé, the group has gone on to enjoy countless demonstrations and participation in a variety of crafts, informal lectures on diverse subjects, table games, shopping trips, tours, plant and recipe exchanges, gourmet luncheons, picnics, holiday parties, and talent shows.

An annual fashion show is among the most popular events. A church member who owns a clothing store readily responded to this idea, offering to outfit anyone willing to model. She also agreed to emcee the show.

It was pouring rain the day of the first show, yet there was a big turnout. In advance, the senior models, male and female, had selected and been fitted with robes, sweaters, skirts and blouses, and jackets. Now they pirouetted on a stage, replete with bamboo screen and potted palms, to the rhythm of sweet music and a lively narration. It was a way of enhancing self-esteem and encouraging older adults to continue to take an interest in their appearance!

What those young adults didn't think of, the senior adults and other church members did to help meet needs in the lives of the older persons in that town. Fresh leadership continues to surface, with imaginative ideas for getting the job done. And countless lives have been blessed, none more than those of us who had a part in getting the program under way.

As we have therefore opportunity,
let us do good unto all men,
especially unto them who are of the household of faith
(Gal. 6:10).

For God is not unrighteous
to forget your work and labour of love,
which ye have shewed toward his name,
in that ye have ministered to the saints,
and do minister (Heb. 6:10).

*

78

OUTSIDE THE hotel dining room in Denver there was a stir of suppressed excitement. Inside, finishing our festive Christmas luncheon, we listened as the director of the children's choir prepared us for what was to come.

"These Hispanic children are economically and culturally disadvantaged youngsters. Practically every one of their families receive public assistance. May I ask one thing of you as an audience? Enter into this experience with them. Smile. Applaud. Sing along. If these children sense that you like them, they will sing their hearts out for you. And don't listen for musical excellence. We sing for the fun of it."

As fifty-five youngsters—ages three through fifteen—marched in, their fringed ponchos flapping, we smiled delightedly. Wrinkled hands that hadn't clapped to a tune in forty years began keeping time to the music. Sophisticated professionals forgot their calendars and thought of Christmas and little children.

Their director was a social worker, their case worker. He and his wife saw a need and met it. Giving after-hours time, they were providing the love, attention, motivation, and small successes that can break the cycle of welfare dependency.

In the Oklahoma City area a minister of music from one church and an organist from another bring the gift of music to more than fifty mentally and/or physically handicapped adults. From every imaginable background, cultured and deprived, with greatly varied capability, they come together each week for an evening of singing and socializing.

The programs they have presented in the Capitol Rotunda, shopping malls, churches, and other places provide the type of group experiences most of them missed while growing up.

These performances give them a special opportunity to make a contribution to life.

Audiences listen with wonder and appreciation, often tearfully, and go away inspired to make better use of their own God-given capabilities. And the families of these special persons say they have been immeasurably blessed.

Both the Denver couple and these two musicians have gone far beyond the call of duty to minister to others. The question is, What, Lord, would you have me do—beyond the call of duty —to bring my caring touch to life?

The best gift you can give others is to make them feel good about themselves.

*

79

FOR ABOUT five years before Mother came to make her home with us I racked my brain for ways to give her a break, a breath of air, a vacation from her daily routine at 111 Oak Street. She was more-or-less homebound, her visits to the homes of her children becoming more and more infrequent, her world gradually shrinking.

Vacation means a change of scene, so each fall we took her on foliage tours. Now, a foliage tour doesn't necessarily require a week in Vermont or even a full day on the Natchez Trace. If your timing is right, a thirty-minute foliage tour of Norman, Oklahoma, like a half-hour spring garden tour of McComb, Mississippi, can be a dream come true.

A minivacation for Mom was often nothing more than a trip to a plant nursery in a neighboring town. Once, after browsing at length in the greenhouses, we got into our car and she discovered she had left her cane at the counter. The cashier laughed when I returned for it.

"It happens all the time," he chuckled. "People come in here and forget all about their ailments." He pointed to a nearby shelf. "Look at that cane over there—it's been here for over a year!"

Not only does vacation mean a change of scene; it means a change of diet, an unexpected treat, a little splurge. Mother would rarely agree to eating out, but she relished the hamburgers and French fries we brought in occasionally. Living only eighty miles away, I often took her frozen home-cooked food she'd never prepare for herself—brisket, sweet and sour chicken, turnip greens, blueberry cake.

Vacation means a good book. For a long time Mother read light romances, and while we sometimes duplicated one (she was quick to tell us when we did!), we provided her with hours of vacation reading. "I love the descriptions of faraway places," she often remarked.

"Vacation" pictures were always welcome—big books filled with photographs of beautiful trees and flowers and landscapes. And postcards—when we moved her, I discovered a veritable history of our travels in her collection of the picture postcards we'd sent her over the years.

Vacations are for seeing family and old friends. On one of Mother's visits to our home we invited cousins she had not seen in years to lunch. They visited to their heart's content while I played maid for the day.

And, of course, vacation means souvenirs. It's marvelous when a parent has a hobby the family can feed through their travels. We have brought plants from far and near, as well as wind chimes and knick-knacks we think she might enjoy.

Vacation means rest from routine, too. When my brother arrived for a visit, he and his wife came bearing great sacks of groceries and declaring the kitchen off limits. Mother talked of these holidays for weeks on end.

As vacation comes to a close, we all start looking to the year ahead. Each year one of the granddaughters makes a sequinned calendar for her. And Mother keeps them, every one, liking nothing better than getting them all out for show and tell. Each is a trophy representing another victorious year, a souvenir of her journey through life.

What does "vacation" mean to you? What kind of vacation would your favorite senior citizen enjoy? Say "See how you are loved" with a vacation treat real soon.

*

80

"HOW ARE things going?" I greeted a church member one Sunday morning. I had heard that her marriage was in serious danger and that her mother's illness had been diagnosed as Alzheimer's.

As we stood aside to let others pass, she poured out her concerns to me. There was little concrete help I could give, but I listened. It was the first of several little "listening" visits we shared in and around the church building.

In a heartfelt message to Christians, a divorcée pled, "We need your T.L.C., your time, your love, your concern." She declared she did not so much need to be told to pray and leave her problems to the Lord, as to have someone throw her arms around her and say, "I hurt for you and love you so much."

Persons in crisis need someone who can give time to in-depth listening, she reminds us. "Confidence grows with time, and with time and the healing of the mind (a long, slow process), constructive reasoning begins to take place.

"Lend us your faith," she cries out, "until ours can be restored."

It's in the long aftermath of crisis, I discovered after our home burned, when the shock of the reality of loss hits, when the difficult decisions must be made, when the endless details must be cared for and life rearranged. I needed to know someone understood that things weren't anywhere near normal for months!

The ministry of listening need not be limited to hurting people. Success, like sorrow, needs to be shared. Listening, we can rejoice with those who rejoice.

In every audience there are the "listening faces," persons whose eyes are alive with interest, whose facial expressions show thoughtfulness or pleasure, whose posture indicates alertness. Listening faces energize and encourage the people on the platform.

Listening to older people recount joys and successes of their past is a ministry, also. Where they grew up, who they married, where they lived, what they did for a living, what about their children, what their hobbies were—wisdom for the living of our own lives is often ours for the asking. Even when there's nothing new to gain from listening, hard as it may be at times, we affirm them in the process.

And, of course, listening to children—instead of hurrying to interrupt or reprimand—we can better minister to their needs. A mother, forced to let her voice rest for weeks, observed, "Silence taught me that the listener is the most important person in any conversation."

A fifty-eight-year-old woman who took a civil service examination and went to work in a San Francisco post office knew her strength as a teacher and friend was in hearing others. As she began to hear the stories of those with whom she worked, she found her concern over her own troubles diminishing. Listening, she grew to love these people from diverse races and backgrounds. And long after she retired, she remained friends with them. "I had gone there thinking the work would distract me, but it had done much more. I had discovered a treasure of affection."

The first duty of love is to listen.

— *Paul Tillich*

*

81

MY FIRST memory of shared caring was the Christmas that Mother let me share with her the joy of "playing Santa Claus." Together, in the evenings after my little sister was asleep, we worked in front of the fireplace in my parents' bedroom.

There were little dresses and gowns to be made from soft batiste for Dorothy's Christmas doll, and sacques and receiving blankets from even softer pink and blue flannelette.

I helped with blanket stitching—pink on blue, blue on pink, while she briarstitched around the tiny necklines of the gowns and dresses, giving each garment a finishing touch of French knots and daisies.

Then, when we finally reached a stopping point, we'd tiptoe through the cold hallway to the guest room, where Mother unlocked the closet and we stored our surprises. (Remembering, I catch a whiff of the red Delicious apples wrapped in purple tissue in the wooden crate Daddy brought home from the store each December.)

I have a few memories of Christmases prior to this one—the year I watched Grandmother making a yellow quilt for my dolls, all the while pretending it was a saddle blanket for Grandpa's horse; the year I had the flu and we had real candles on our Christmas tree (I shudder to think of Daddy's lighting them!); the year Santa brought me a little desk and my Aunt Harriet gave me a little hatbox filled with pecans.

But none are so precious as the experience of helping my mother prepare for Dorothy's Christmas morning.

Likewise, there may be no greater gift that we can give others than when we help them bring their caring touch to life. We can watch for a spark of interest, for latent capabilities and resources. We may ask them to come along and help us. Or we become enablers, saying, "Bring me your children" or "Here, take this check—you go and minister."

We may be used of God in igniting their gift of service. We can encourage them to treasure and develop their spiritual gift. Our affirmation may be the nudge that turns a natural instinct for caring into glory.

Sometimes we may be able to help a dream become reality. There are people with a vision of a ministry who cannot seem to "find a handle," to know just how and where to begin.

For example, here's a woman who wants to teach someone to read. She does not know where to begin. She needs training. She needs to know how to make herself available to an illiterate person. She may never fulfill her heart's desire unless she gets in touch with a person or a group dedicated to literacy training.

A busy woman working in Denver's inner city taught a Sunday School class for older adults in addition to supervising a lively weekday program involving volunteers. I asked her how she managed to handle this class along with her other responsibilities.

"When I hear of a class member who needs attention, I ask another member to call and check on her."

In her class as well as her weekday program, she helps others bring their caring touch to life.

Ministry is every Christian's job, and we deprive another of a sense of fulfillment and the joy that comes from service when we think we must do it all ourselves.

Actually, we minister as we help others bring their caring touch to life.

The Christian is not only a person who becomes a partner with God in creation; he is also a person who tries to help other people to do the same.

— *D. Elton Trueblood*

*

82

THERE'S SCARCELY anything more appreciated than a heartwarming story of someone's caring touch. An acquaintance gave me such a story several years ago, and it is among my most cherished Christmas gifts.

She was the mother of three young children. Her husband had abandoned the family and she was struggling along, without financial support from him, trying to make ends meet while taking courses to prepare herself for the working world. It was getting on toward Christmas and Marianne (I'll call her that) didn't know what she was going to do about Christmas for her kids.

She had a lot on her mind—her father was in the hospital, her sister's first baby was due, and always there was studying—when she received a call from a Mrs. Shands.

"I'd like to take you shopping for your kids," she said. Marianne agreed, without much enthusiasm. She was tired, physically and mentally. Like a broken record, the thought kept repeating itself, ". . . but *I* have nothing . . . nothing . . . to give this year."

Now, add to that, thoughts of going out to spend someone else's money—shopping with a total stranger. She racked her brain for ideas of inexpensive items for each child. She didn't sleep too well that night.

Fixing breakfast the next day, she recalled that the stranger had said something about groceries and she took a quick inventory—half a box of cereal, half a gallon of milk, some canned goods, and two weeks to go before more food stamps.

Promptly at ten on the morning of Christmas Eve Mrs. Shands was at the door, slender, smiling, her expensive white car parked in front of the house. She admired pictures of the children while an uneasy Marianne got her coat.

In the car, however, the two were soon chatting away like old friends. Mrs. Shands, too, had suffered a broken marriage. She, too, had gone back to school.

Several years ago, she explained, her teenage son had died in an automobile accident. Since then, each Christmas she and her husband used the money they would have spent for his gifts to do something for others.

Still, this venture was hard on Marianne. Anxious and jittery, she stammered when Mrs. Shands asked if she wanted to give the children clothes or toys.

As they went into the store Marianne finally gathered courage to ask, "Can you give me an idea of what your budget has in store for this project? I don't want to take advantage of you or anything." She really felt awkward.

It was a very, very generous amount that Mrs. Shands calmly named, and Marianne stammered, "O-o-o-h, I wasn't expecting anything like that!" She was thrilled, but it was hard on her. She just wasn't used to spending someone else's money!

Mrs. Shands grinned and took off for the toy department. When Marianne paused uncertainly to look at price tags on airplanes and shoe skates, Mrs. Shands threw them into their basket. As they browsed through the store, she added coloring books, games, underwear, socks, gloves, sweaters, toy dishes, play makeup and a little make-up box, paper, tape, ribbons.

And then to the grocery store, where it was, "Do you like this? . . . Oh, get the kids some of this . . . Let's go up and down the aisles. Get what you want or need. Do you need this . . . this . . . this?" Mrs. Shands was having a great time. The tab came to over $130!

Back at the house, Marianne felt a kind of sadness. Their visit was almost over. When they got everything unloaded, Mrs. Shands turned and gave Marianne a big hug and said, "Merry Christmas!"

As Marianne tried to thank her, Mrs. Shands just smiled real big and was gone.

Inside, walking around among the sacks of Christmas

goodies, as the impact of the past two hours hit Marianne, the tears rolled. It was like a dream.

There wasn't time for wrapping gifts before the children returned, so she sorted everything out in groups under the Christmas tree . . . Mark, Laura, Jennifer . . . and hurried to get them, and her mother, too.

They had no idea they were about to experience a true Christmas. "Wait in the car a minute." Marianne ran to get her camera and motioned them in.

Now here they came . . . their eyes bugged . . . there was a stunned silence . . . and then the squeals.

"Oh, thank you, Mom. Oh, thanks, Mom," they kept saying.

"These aren't from me."

"But who? The family? The church? Mom, *you* bought *these!*" They were really puzzled.

"The Lord provided them for you, children."

"Aw, Mom, you *did* it."

"No, the Lord provided all this through a lady, a total stranger to us. I never met her until this morning." And as she began to tell the story, the joy and gratitude just flowed and they began asking, "A stranger? Maybe the wife of a TV star? Someone rich?"

The story of the "Strange Lady" who came to their door on Christmas Eve was the highlight of the children's Christmas. They bubbled to tell their family and friends. All were astounded.

And as Marianne shared the story of their special Christmas she realized she had something to give, after all, "a gift from the Lord Himself," she said.

"As I told the story over and over to those dear to us, there were tears in their eyes as well as mine. And their thank-you was in their grateful response, "Marianne, you've *made* my Christmas!"

*

And I pray that Christ will be more and more at home in your hearts, living within you as you trust in him. May your roots go down deep into the soil of God's marvelous love; and may you be able to feel and understand, as all God's children should, how long, how wide, how deep, and how high his love really is (Eph. 3:17-18, TLB).

Yes, may you come to know his love—although it can never be fully known—and so be completely filled with the very nature of God (v. 19, GNB).

AFTERNOONS
WITH
MISS BETTY

MASCOT
B O O K S
an imprint of Amplify Publishing Group

www.mascotbooks.com

Afternoons with Miss Betty: Life Lessons and Wisdom Inspired by My Dog

For more information, please contact:
Mascot Books, an imprint of Amplify Publishing Group
620 Herndon Parkway, Suite 220
Herndon, VA 20170
info@mascotbooks.com

Library of Congress Control Number: 2023914792

CPSIA Code: PRV1123A
ISBN-13: 978-1-63755-899-7

Printed in the United States

To Tony + Anna
Good FRIENDS
Enjoy ?

Don Rose

To my dog, Miss Betty,

and all those out there who love their dogs.

Don Rose

AFTERNOONS WITH MISS BETTY

Life Lessons and Wisdom
Inspired by My Dog

CONTENTS

Chapter 1

MISS BETTY

Miss Betty is definitely a little girl. Weighing in at twenty pounds, with a back height of eight inches, she is a petite-size labradoodle and will not get bigger. She has a soft caramel-brown coat, with a bit of white on top of her head, as well as white "socks" on her feet. Her eyes are a warm brown, and when I look into them, I melt.

She was the first one born in her litter, but she ended up being the runt.

When we first saw her, the breeder said there were two dogs to pick from: Miss Betty and another beautiful puppy.

How to choose, how to select a "new" member of your family, how to commit to raising this puppy from now until her passing?

It was not easy, but the answer was given to us. Miss Betty was gentle, a baby girl needing protection, love, and warm arms to hold her. We had all that and more.

I particularly felt the need and want to protect this vulnerable, young, innocent, tiny bundle of joy. She was grateful to be hugged warmly and returned the kindness with lots of kisses.

I was taught by my gentle father that one should treat women and girls with total respect and equal status. I have always followed those lessons, and even today, after thirty-four years of marriage, I open the car door for my wife every time.

I found myself looking at this tiny, warm, little girl dog wanting me to be her everything. She also had my wife, Jenny, who loves Miss Betty and chose her name, and her buddy, Uncle Frank—her forty-pound, four-years-older labradoodle big brother.

I love Uncle Frank, and you might have read my book *Mornings with Uncle Frank*, which details how our relationship developed and continues to flourish today.

I titled this book *Afternoons with Miss Betty* because in the afternoons, when we are all a bit tired, there is Miss Betty, *demanding* we all go for a walk. We go, are invigorated, and are always glad we went. "Thanks, Miss Betty," we all say as we slump into our chairs after a big, cool drink of water. Bringing Miss Betty into our home, our lives, and our hearts has been a blessing, and we love our little puppy.

Our days are full in our Carmel-by-the-Sea home in California. Our schedule includes a lot of outdoor time. We breathe the fresh air, and all is well in our world.

Miss Betty has brought a lot into our lives, from that new-puppy energy, the addition of a new family member, to another wonderful body to love. We enjoy dinnertime, treat time, and just being with each other time. A wonderful world, indeed, thanks to this tiny, small bundle of love.

Chapter 2

MY SHADOW

I never have to look for Miss Betty in the afternoons, because she is always around my feet. She is a labradoodle, which is a mix of Labrador and poodle. These dogs come in three sizes: petite, medium, and standard. Miss Betty is a petite dog of twenty pounds. By my feet is where she is always found. I call her my shadow, which makes my wife a bit crazy. "I'm the one who wanted a second dog. If it wasn't for me, you would not be here," she often tells Miss Betty, thinking that Miss Betty might be appreciative and want to be around her more often.

But *no*. Miss Betty is my buddy.

I think the reason is that I "love" her.

I treat her with respect; she is definitely a girl, and I feel a need to protect her. She is a small dog—another reason for me to protect her. At night, as we are sitting on the couch watching TV, Miss Betty climbs up on the couch and nestles next to me, with my arm sitting on top of her, gently rubbing her as she sleeps. She often turns on her back in a contorted way and even snores.

If I am into the TV program and ignoring her, she gets up and goes to sleep under a side table. Her condo, I call it.

But if I get up for a glass of water or for any reason, she is right there by my feet—my shadow. I am amazed at how she can go from asleep to fully awake, wanting to go wherever I am going.

If I go into the garage to get a tool, Miss Betty has got to go with me. Even as I open the garage door, I hold it for an additional beat because I know Miss Betty is by my feet and going into the garage with me.

I am always saying, "Where's my little girl?" even when I know she is right there with me.

Several times a day, I just stop what I am doing to look into her eyes, give her a good rub, and tell her, "You're a good girl, Miss Betty." She loves that, and so do I. I think it's important to tell those you love that you love them every chance you get. Our time on this planet is finite, and one day you will not be able to say those words. Miss Betty knows she is loved and is an important member of this family.

Do I get tired of her always being by my feet? *No*, not one bit, even when she steps on my heels to let me know she is there.

It is actually an honor to know someone loves you and is unafraid to show it. As I type these words, Miss Betty is on my left side, by my feet, sleeping but ready to spring to life if I move more than an inch from this chair.

When someone loves you, it feels good, and it is important to nurture that relationship and return the love. Miss Betty teaches me to be aware of the people in my life who I want to tell that they are important and loved. It is not easy to tell my friends I love them at the end of a phone call, but I do it, and they often respond in kind.

Chapter 3

DOGS

I wonder how it came to be that I have such affection for my two dogs: Uncle Frank and Miss Betty.

When I was growing up, animals were not an important part of our family. We had a parakeet, but it was really my mom's. We did little maintenance, if any, and barely acknowledged the bird. I have no idea what its name was. Skipper, maybe?

I was consumed with school, after-school sports, my friends, and Boy Scouts. I had little time for pets. As I got older, it was home life, school life, and work life.

My college years were busy, and then I got caught up in the life that I would live: marriage, four kids, running a company for forty years, and then retirement.

Family life was wonderful, with soccer, flag football, cheerleading, volleyball, flag girl practices, and all the friends my children had. Busy, busy, but absolutely the best of times. Summer vacations, camping, family camps, Hawaii, and all the while no or few pets. My kids tell me we had a dog for a short while, but I'll be darned if I can remember a dog.

After the kids were out on their own, and we were comfortable being retired, my wife decided we "needed" a dog, so we adopted Riley, a cute little bichon that was every inch *a terror.* The dang thing nipped at every person who ever came into our house.

That dog was tiny, but such a pain to own. My wife would disagree, and that's because Riley only liked—or should I say loved—her. The rest of us were in the way and needed to be bitten.

When Riley was kind of on his last legs, my wife again said, "We need another dog for Riley to be friends with."

"Oh really?" I replied.

My wife is persistent, if anything, and here comes a little reddish-brown, medium-size labradoodle, cute as can be.

"That's my dog," I proclaimed. "I get to name it, and I want it to like *me.*"

So, to amuse myself, I named him Uncle Frank. Everyone needs an uncle, right?

So Uncle Frank came to live with us and his rotten brother—I mean, that nice little dog Riley.

Within the year, Riley had passed away. I do miss him—a little. No one has been bitten around here since his passing.

Uncle Frank turned out to be a bright, shining light in our lives, and for the first time in my life, I had a dog. A dog that liked me, a dog that I could be pals with, and a true animal friend. I can say it out loud: "I love Uncle Frank."

After a few years, my wife again said, "We need a buddy for Uncle Frank. Let's get another labradoodle, but a smaller size."

"OK," I said, "but I'm concerned we are going to end up with a Riley personality."

So we carefully looked at the puppies and found a sweet, cute, tiny, adorable one that was just right. And so Miss Betty came to live with us.

A wonderful addition to our family.

Miss Betty was a personality overload. As soon as she got through the puppy stage, she became the dominant dog in the house. Sorry, Uncle Frank. Thank goodness Uncle Frank is twice as big as Miss Betty and always will be. He does not have to deal with her when he doesn't want to; he just jumps to a higher space or coolly ignores her.

Now we have two dogs, and I wouldn't have it any other way. I am now a dog person. After having Uncle Frank for seven years and Miss Betty for three years, we are bonded for life.

When non–dog people visit our house, I keep a close eye on Uncle Frank and Miss Betty—no jumping or barking or anything to scare our guests. Most people are dog people and greet both Uncle Frank and Miss Betty with enthusiasm.

It is funny that I lived my entire life without an appreciation for animals, and now I am a total animal person.

I didn't dislike animals; I just did not feel any connection to them. I loved the wild animals I saw on TV and in documentaries. I did not relate to dogs or cats; I felt no need to pet them or to talk to them. I just ignored them.

When I see people ignore my dogs, I get it. But I really do enjoy it when people come into my yard or house and acknowledge my dogs, get down to their level, and talk kindly to them.

They are my people.

We all need to be exposed to different things—to broaden our perspectives. It took me a lifetime to love animals and feel something for them. I missed out on many years of loving a pet, enjoying a pet, and feeling the love back.

We all need to get out of our comfort zone sometimes. I'm so glad I did.

Chapter 4

SEASONS

We decided to move to the Sierra Nevada town of Reno, Nevada, on a two-and-one-half-acre property in 2021 after living in the resort town of Carmel, California, on a beautiful but small property for seventeen years. We were looking for a new environment and weather that changed more than ten degrees all year long. Carmel was heaven, but we were ready for a change of pace. Life is only so long, and you must taste as much as you can, within reason.

Hey! I'm getting away from "Seasons."

Reno, Nevada, where we now live, has four definite seasons, and moving from Carmel with Miss Betty has been an eye-opening experience.

Summer, fall, winter, and spring are distinct seasons from each other.

During the summer, we have about three months of weather in which the temperatures stay in the low to midnineties every day. It is hot, so I do not walk Miss Betty on the hot asphalt trails in the area. The other day, I took her out to a rustic dirt path that we often use for walking. I can let Miss Betty off-leash, and she has the freedom to run and explore. I keep walking along the path, and Miss Betty does not let me get too far out of her sight.

On this dirt trail, there are three different paths, all of different lengths. We take the middle-length path, and Miss Betty is having fun, as usual. Remember: this is a pretty hot day, in the midnineties. Miss Betty gets ahead of me, then just stops in a shaded area. As I walk up to her, she is not her usual self and looks pooped. She is overheated. I pick her up, and she seems relaxed and happy to be in my arms. I carry her for a while, when she lets me know she wants down. We go straight home, and once inside our air-conditioned house, she goes right for the water. She was too hot on the walk. I must remember to take either short walks during the day or take her out only when the sun has set.

I keep her cool during the summer and watch her carefully to make sure she is getting enough water and minimal sun exposure.

Fall here is wonderful, with all the trees going deciduous with a burst of yellows, reds, and oranges—a beautiful time of year and a cooling-off period. Walking Miss Betty can take place any time of the day. Cool winds blow, and we start bracing for winter. A truly spectacular view from our hilltop house looking down into the Reno Valley.

Winter is always a surprise. We go to sleep at night, only to find a winter wonderland in the morning. The soft snowflakes drift down as if in a musical. Before we know it, there are six to eight inches on the ground. Miss Betty cautiously walks out the front door to find snow up to her belly.

At first she is unsure, but then her memory of past winters kicks in, and she runs around our courtyard as if possessed. Big circles, then a quick skid, then big hops in the fun white clouds that envelope our yard. She is in heaven, with snow all over her, her face white with joy. She does her "duty," then comes inside. But before I can let her into our warm house, I have to get all the tiny snowballs off her belly, head, and body. Sometimes it is so full I need to get the hair dryer and sit with her while the warm air turns her back into my Miss Betty.

Winter is a fun and challenging time of year. Time for her to wear coats outside and even inside sometimes. She loves running like crazy in the backyard, going from here to there at rocket speed. You can almost hear her laughing the entire time. Then I warm her up and get all the snow off her coat. I change her coat, then love it as she snuggles next to me in my big leather chair and falls asleep by my side as I read a book.

Spring is an exciting time of year, as the snow begins to disappear, and the trees begin to show foliage. Soft linden green leaves first appear, then spring explodes, and there is color everywhere. The Reno Valley is a burst of yellow, green, purple, and flowers of every color of the rainbow. Life is beginning again in the Sierra Nevada.

Miss Betty is also lively, running here and there. It is important work she does looking for lizards, chasing squirrels, and watching the quail eating seed in our yard. Soon they will be running with the dad quail on lookout, and Mom and the dust-ball kids run to keep up. It's a wonderful sight.

Miss Betty is experiencing life in the mountains and loving it. She has a large fenced-in yard to dominate, more territory than she can comfortably control. She follows me everywhere

I walk in the yard; she drifts off for any movement, then gets back in line.

We have a wonderful life here, and I think Miss Betty is in love with her family and her life.

It's important to create a life you can enjoy—to find a place you can grow, experience the seasons, and appreciate what you have. The things you have now are the things you prayed for long ago. Learn to appreciate what you have and where you are. A lesson for us all.

Chapter 5

BATHROOM AT NIGHT

Miss Betty is a small dog and does not have the capacity to "hold it" all night.

But neither do I.

Miss Betty sleeps next to me at night, which I do not mind, because she is small and easily fits in the arch of my legs.

At some point each night, she gets out of bed and goes to the bedroom door. At first she softly cries to get my attention. I am a pretty heavy sleeper and do not hear her first attempts at waking me up. From the depths of my slumber, I begin to hear her crying, which is much louder now. As I slowly regain consciousness, I wonder why my wife, Jenny, never hears Miss Betty's cries. I think I know why.

I am up and almost to the door before I even know I'm awake.

Miss Betty wags her tail and waits for me to open the bedroom door and then the front door as we walk out into the enclosed front courtyard.

I turn on the lights and let Miss Betty do her business.

I wait in a standing sleep mode until Miss Betty is back at the door. I turn off the lights, shut the door, and head back to my warm bed.

Miss Betty is waiting for me on the bed and gives me a couple of good licks to let me know she appreciates my efforts on her behalf.

I enjoy the thanks, but I need to get back to sleep. I pull up the covers, and Miss Betty lies by my bent knees to fall back asleep.

This is our nightly routine. But sometimes the routine changes.

We live in the Sierra Nevada mountains, and we often get very strong winds that howl through our property.

One night, Miss Betty had to go outside. I turned on the outdoor lights and opened the door for her to go out, but the wind was so strong and shocking to Miss Betty that she jumped back in as if to say, "No, no, no."

Remember: I was half-asleep, but I laughed at this innocent small dog's refusal to go out in this windstorm.

I walked her back to my closet, turned on the light, put on slippers and my bathrobe, and walked Miss Betty to the front door. "No way," she said with her pretty brown eyes. I reassured her, gently picked her up, and headed out into this nine-hundred-mile-per-hour gale. It was hard to even close the door. I took her out to the four-foot wall that surrounds our courtyard and set her down as close to the wall as possible. Here the wall blocked the wind, providing a bit of calm.

She got it and quickly went to the bathroom, then looked to me for advice. The winds were too strong, so I picked her up in my arms. Together we fought our way back to the front door. Inside, the wind was gone, and a happy Miss Betty ran back to our bed. This time I got a multitude of *love licks*, thanking me for all the help. I appreciated it, but I was tired. I pulled up the blankets, and Miss Betty went to her spot. Off to sleep we went after our big adventure.

Sometimes our daily routines are disrupted, and it is important to work together to navigate the change. Disruption can be an adventure, and these adventures really begin at the end of our comfort zone. Life begins at the end of your comfort zone. Life is the acquisition of memories. Don't leave this life with dreams unfulfilled, but with memories for you and all you touch in this life.

Chapter 6

OUR WALK

Sometimes I think Miss Betty should be called my nurse, physical therapist, or doctor because she demands an afternoon walk every day—a routine we both need.

On most days, I give myself a break from activities and take a nap around two in the afternoon. I just sit back in my chair in the family room and drift off to sleep. Miss Betty also takes a nap at this time, either on my lap or on the side of my chair, where my hand can softly rub her while we both relax. Soon we are both asleep in the warm afternoon sun. It is a very pleasant time indeed.

At some point, Miss Betty ends up on the floor and seems content.

She allows me to take my break, but at three o'clock each day she begins to stir and softly cries to wake me up. I really don't mind, because I only want between forty-five minutes to an hour to rest. That is all I need and all I want. But the soft crying drags me up from that wonderful sleep, and I resist as much as

I can at first. The crying gets louder and more demanding, then I wake up. I'm not fully awake, but I'm out of sleep mode.

Miss Betty wants to go for our afternoon walk, but she wants to go now! I let her know I need more time to wake up. I need my legs to work and my mouth to be able to form words. Then I am awake. I am not sure I want to go for a long walk, but I know it is good for my health, and Miss Betty is demanding. I go to the mud room, where I keep her leash, and Miss Betty is so excited because she knows we are heading out. Her tail wags her whole body with excitement.

I sit on the outdoor bench to put on her leash. She knows to sit in front of me while I put it on. Once the leash is on, and doggie bags are in my pocket for you-know-what, off we go.

Miss Betty is on full alert for any lizards napping on a warm rock, and she looks at every rock intently. We walk up the rustic dirt path far from the streets and in a high-desert environment.

When I am sure we are safe, I often let Miss Betty off-leash so she can have some freedom and control over where she goes. She is on the hunt and goes this way and that way. She often pokes her head up to see where I am. Once assured I am close, off she goes. She often gets ahead of me or behind me, then runs like the wind to get near me to check in.

I wonder if she is mocking me or simply teasing me. Off-leash, she is fast. She thinks her four legs are a real benefit and laughs that I only have two legs. And I must admit—she is definitely faster than me. As I struggle to go up a fairly steep slope, my breathing increases, and I begin to slow down. She just breezes past me, going up and down the slope at a blinding speed. The slope seems to have no effect on her. I think I see her laughing at me, but I'm not sure. "OK! OK! You are faster than me," I say, and that seems to satisfy her for the moment.

She loves the freedom of being off-leash, to run and to explore, and to see the world around her.

A bigger dog was walking by us with their owner, and Miss Betty was just so anxious to meet the other dog that she ran right up to it and gave a double bark. The other dog gave a much louder and deeper bark.

Miss Betty came screaming back to me in a flash. "What the hell was that thing?" she seemed to say. "Thank God I have my quick four feet. That thing was going to eat me."

On the way home, she walked with a bit of an attitude, with her head held high. *I met the enemy, and I'm still here.*

When we got closer to home, and all was safe, I continued to leave her off-leash. She ran like the wind down to the bottom of the hill and along the sidewalk. She knows not to cross the street without me, but she is showing off her speed. "Come on, two-feet, hurry up," she says.

Miss Betty is my great walking buddy, and I love that she has more legs. Our walks seem just right, and I wouldn't have it any other way.

This has become a sacred part of our day. Even though I'm initially hesitant to go because I want more sleep, I know Miss Betty is looking out for me.

So yes, Miss Betty is my nurse, physical therapist, and doctor.

In life, we often need someone to push us—to make us do what we don't want to do but know we should. We need a friend looking out for our best interests.

We also need to be that friend who helps and pushes others.

Chapter 7

NICKNAMES

Miss Betty has a lot of nicknames. I call her Miss Betty most of the time, but when she is outside, sometimes I call her Short Stack or Shrimp Boat. "Come on in, Short Stack," I say.

She is just so cute and sweet that I attach nicknames that reflect her personality—names of endearment.

I do think Miss Betty is an appropriate name for her—a bit of high class and a bit of English proper. Maybe a bit of southern charm. I can almost hear people saying, "Why, hello, Miss Betty. How are you on this fine day?"

We're more laid-back, so we just say, "What's up, Miss Betty?"

I often call her Little Girl. "Come on, Little Girl. Let's go outside," or, "Hey, Little Girl, want a chicken treat?"

To me, she is all these things, and I say them with respect and love. But almost like having a child, *sometimes* when I say Miss Betty, she knows I am not messing around and that I mean business.

"Miss Betty, get over here." When said with authority, she

knows I mean *now*.

Often that is because she might be in some sort of danger from a car or getting too far away from me on a walk when she is allowed to be leash-free.

Every morning she just stares at me when I start to wake up, waiting for me to pet her and say, "Good morning, Miss Betty," or, "Morning, Little Girl."

There are not too many popular names that start with *Miss*. There is Miss Kitty, on the old TV show *Gunsmoke*, which most people don't know; there's Miss America, but that is a title; and then there are the *Miss* book titles, like *Little Miss Bossy* and *Little Miss Naughty*, but those are *Little Miss*, not *Miss*. So Miss Betty's name is unique, and people seem to love it when she is introduced. "What a pretty name for a pretty girl," they say as they give her a little head rub when they first meet her.

Miss Betty proudly wears her name, and I can't even imagine her without her special name.

All names are special, and to be called by your name and have a nickname is fun. My daughters—Krista, Holly, and Madison—I call KR, Holly Beth, and Mo, respectively. I call my son, Joel, JC. Nicknames are earned by having a close relationship with someone and an endearing, special name. After watching an Austin Powers film, my daughter Madison decided my name should be Baj. What? Baj? But from ten years old, she never called me Dad again. Always called me Baj, sent cards to me as Baj, and all her friends call me Baj. Even my young granddaughter calls me Papa Baj. Life is funny.

Chapter 8

RETURN

I had the privilege of meeting with our good friends from Southern California, who invited us on a three-day trip to Carmel and Monterey, California, to play golf at Spyglass and the world-famous Pebble Beach Golf Links.

We lived in Carmel for seventeen years before moving to Reno, Nevada, so we are familiar with the central coast, and this would be our first time back since we moved in 2021. We decided to extend our trip an additional three days so we could meet with our wonderful neighbors who we left behind physically, but with whom we kept up phone calls and emails.

The golf was magical, with perfect weather, a great foursome, and some good and not-so-good shots. I must admit, playing two long courses in two days was more than I could comfortably handle. By the fifteenth hole of each course, I was beat. Personally, I think golf should be fifteen holes; however, I pushed on and played respectable for holes fifteen through eighteen. Tired or not, one does not give up on these elite golf courses, especially

Pebble Beach. I took a photo with my friend Bob and told him, "We will look at this photo when we are sitting in rocking chairs on a deck in the future and remember the wonderful time we had playing Pebble Beach." I'm pretty sure our scores will get better over the years. I might even have more birdies than I really had. Ha ha! Time will tell.

After the three days, I was tired and missing my Miss Betty and Uncle Frank, but we scheduled another three days to meet up with our neighbor friends. We stayed at the Mission Ranch, owned by Clint Eastwood, the actor and director, which is located in a scenic area of Carmel. We met with our friends at restaurants, in their houses, and at wine bars. So wonderful to catch up, especially with Frank Southers, who is a real author of many incredible books, and we had a good talk.

It was great to be back in Carmel, and we enjoyed the many good restaurants, coffeehouses, stores, and sights.

A wonderful time.

When it was time to end our adventure, we packed up, and off we went on the six-hour drive back home.

During our trip to Carmel, our dog sitter, Sarah, sent us photos of Uncle Frank and Miss Betty, our labradoodles. Uncle Frank is a medium-size labradoodle, and he has been with us four years longer than Miss Betty. He is the sweetest dog, with big brown eyes and a wonderful disposition. The photos showed them laying around the house, playing in the backyard, and taking walks.

We knew when we got home we would get an exuberant welcome from our dogs. As we got closer, we talked about being with our dogs again, and we both admitted we really missed them.

We pulled up to the driveway. They were both sitting in the front courtyard. *Sitting* is the wrong word; they were going crazy in the front courtyard. We quickly got out of the car and rushed through the gates to an onslaught of licking and loving from our two dogs. Jumping, crying, and yelps of joy. It is a special feeling to be loved so much, and the love went both ways. Our return was fantastic. If people could openly display the love these two dogs demonstrated, we would have a better world. Uncle Frank and Miss Betty have taught me to be more open about my feelings to my friends and family. When I plan to meet my family and friends, I now write to them, "Can't wait to see you," and when I see them, I show a modified display of affection by giving them a big, long-lasting hug, as I was taught by Uncle Frank and Miss Betty.

Your dogs have no filters; they have unabashed, pure feelings. They don't hold back. They don't pretend. They are fully transparent. We can learn from this. I want those around me to know how important they are to me. No filters, no holding back. When I am gone, I want them to know how important we were to each other. My life is made better with them in it.

Chapter 9

SCHOOLTIME

Miss Betty was ready for some education, so we signed her up for ZoomRoom, a dog training facility.

Miss Betty loves other dogs, so when the class began filling up, she was delirious with excitement to see all the other dogs of different breeds and sizes.

This was not socialization training but command training, so interaction was not encouraged. When Miss Betty understood this message, she settled down and prepared for the task at hand.

The basic "sit" command was easy for Miss Betty. I thought, "We have this. My smart dog is going to ace this class."

Little did I know, some of the commands were difficult for all the dogs, and Miss Betty was no exception. She struggled a bit. But as the weeks progressed, and with a lot of homework, she began to excel. Training Miss Betty took patience and consistency, and with her energy at a high level, that was quite a task, but a fun time for both of us, with her abilities beginning to show. She was proud to show off her new skills.

During the fifth class, the trainers wanted to see how each dog was progressing, so they devised a test. All dogs were to stand, sit, lay down, sit again, and stand. In a thirty-second window, they were to do as many of these five commands in a row as they could. To me, this seemed monumental, and I was unsure if Miss Betty could understand and perform all these commands.

The thirty seconds started, and Miss Betty went to work. Afterward, the instructor went to each dog owner and quietly asked, "How many did your dog do?"

"Eight," I said, proudly.

There were eight dogs in the class, and we tied with another dog. We were very proud, and I let Miss Betty know she did great.

But the instructor said we needed a tiebreaker. Everyone would watch as the two dogs and their owners repeated the process. Oh, joy!

"Go!" said the instructor.

Miss Betty began to quickly go through the motions.

At the end of the contest, the instructor again came around and asked, "How many repetitions?"

"Eight," I said quietly, for no reason.

The other dog did seven.

We won! Way to go, Miss Betty. Way to go.

The instructor gave us a twenty-five-dollar gift certificate to be used at the ZoomRoom store.

We were very proud, but I have to reiterate that Miss Betty is a small, twenty-pound dog. For her to stand, sit, lay, and repeat was not too hard, because she is so low to the ground, and the other dog was definitely bigger and thus had more ground to cover. But hey, we didn't make the rules.

Miss Betty proudly left the class with a spring in her step, her head held high, and a twenty-five-dollar gift certificate.

When challenged, you must try your best. If Miss Betty had come in last place, it would have been OK. She tried; she did it. We all face adversity, and we must meet these challenges head-on. We learn best through effort and even failure.

Failure teaches us a lot about ourselves. When we fail, we learn and grow stronger, using that lesson to learn. Life is all about learning and growing.

Sketch by Adrienne Ormsby Pereira

Chapter 10

ALONE

Miss Betty is my buddy, and she is always underfoot, in a good way. Whenever I call out, "Miss Betty, where are you?" all I have to do is look around my feet, and there she is. One would think I could remember that, but she is so small and most of the time at my heel, so I don't immediately see her.

Whenever I leave with my wife on some type of errand, I don't worry too much about Miss Betty, because she is with Uncle Frank, and I know they will both be safe—they have each other. That is one of the reasons we got a second dog: to make sure neither dog is ever lonely.

But occasionally, when Uncle Frank needs to go to the veterinarian or the groomer, we have to leave Miss Betty alone. She senses we are leaving, and when she sees Uncle Frank on a leash and not her, she begins to panic. It makes me feel terrible to see Miss Betty so upset.

Just today we were hanging out around the house, doing chores and enjoying each other, when I had to take Uncle Frank to his grooming appointment. My wife was staying home, so Miss Betty should have been more comfortable, but she was not. She did not like that I was leaving without her. She panicked and started crying. It kills me when Miss Betty cries. My grandchildren in Louisiana would cry when they were young when we left after a visit. We, our children, and our grandchildren all had tears in our eyes, and no one could actually talk. We were all sad to see each other go. Such a feeling of sadness. But we all had to get back to our lives, and we did get together with such great joy to see each other again and again.

Miss Betty made my heart hurt when I took Uncle Frank out through the garage door into the car. I could hear Miss Betty scratching at the door and crying.

My wife said, "Just go. Miss Betty will be OK."

I knew that to be true, but for a few seconds, I was devastated.

Miss Betty couldn't go with me and Uncle Frank, because she is too small, and I couldn't give them both attention on our way to the appointment.

After I returned without Uncle Frank, she was nothing but euphoric when she saw me walk into the house. She cried tears of joy!

When the groomer called, and I had to go back to pick up a handsome Uncle Frank, Miss Betty better understood that I would be gone for a bit, but I would return before too long. She felt better about staying home with Mom.

I am an emotional guy, and my heart easily goes out to children and animals, especially my dogs.

So, when they are upset, I am upset.

I try to include my dogs in all things I do around the house and am constantly saying, "Let's go, guys," or, "Dad's going to the backyard. Who's coming with me?" Miss Betty is *always* a yes, and Uncle Frank makes up his own mind in the afternoons. In the mornings, Uncle Frank is always a yes too.

I think it's funny that I refer to myself as *Dad* to my dogs, and my wife is *Mom*.

It seems natural, as I was Dad to all my children. Actually, my daughter Holly always called me Pop, but you know what I mean.

To refer to myself as *Dad* seems right. I wonder what other pet owners call themselves. I think they all do! It would seem wrong to call myself *Don* to the dogs. I see them as my responsibility, same as my children. I see myself as their teacher of right and wrong and life lessons. It is my duty to feed them, make sure they get rest, and regularly take them to the vet and groomer, not unlike my four children.

Dad seems personable and shows my close relationship with my dogs. I rarely even see them as dogs; I see them as Uncle Frank and Miss Betty. Their personalities are different and unique. They have different needs and wants, and I make sure those differences are taken care of as needed.

Whenever I leave home for multiple days, I truly miss my buddies. When Miss Betty is vocal about it, I have an inner cry when I leave and a loud, vocal cry of joy when I return home.

Missing someone, even for a short time, is a sign of a healthy relationship. Sharing your life is a wonderful thing. People and animals alike all want to be loved and missed. We all enjoy getting together with loved ones. That is what life is all about. I am so thankful for my family, my friends, and my Uncle Frank and Miss Betty.

Chapter 11

HAWAII TRIP

When our four children grew up and started getting married and having children of their own, Jenny and I decided that instead of buying birthday, anniversary, Christmas, and other holiday presents, we would only buy gifts for the grandchildren for all events.

But we would take the entire family—our children, their spouses, and their children—on an all-inclusive trip to Hawaii every five years.

We found a delightful hotel right on the beach in Maui, where every family had their own condominium with a beautiful view of the ocean, aquatic life, and the breathtaking sunset at the end of each day.

Jenny and I would rent the only larger unit available, where we could all congregate and have drinks, food, and just hang around each other.

We have done this for twenty years, and it is the highlight of our family's time together. Ten days of interacting, loving, going on adventures, or relaxing—no pressure to do anything.

We all leave from different parts of the country to meet in Maui. Krista and her family travel from Louisiana; Holly and her family, as well as Joel and his family, both from Central California; and Jenny and I from Nevada.

Our last trip was in June 2015.

One very major and tragic difference in this trip was that our youngest daughter, Madison, could not be there. She was killed in August 2015 in a traffic accident. Our hearts will never recover. She died just after our last family trip, in 2015. It will be interesting to see how we all react in this sacred place we have been coming to for all these years without her large, fun, inclusive-type personality.

It had been seven years, and we all seemed to have survived, but we are not without major scars, tears, and memories. She is never far from our thoughts, and there will be stories and many toasts in her honor.

This brings me to a much smaller but still real problem: we would be without Uncle Frank and Miss Betty for ten days.

I was afraid Miss Betty would be very sad that we were gone, but especially for me. She is my little buddy. Our relationship is strong, and we do a lot together each day. Ten days! That is a long time for a small dog, even for me. I would miss our interactions. We had a wonderful dog sitter, Sarah, who stayed in our house. Uncle Frank would be there, and Sarah brought her small dog, Whiskey, whom both our dogs enjoy, especially Miss Betty, who is about the same size. Sarah says it is a vacation for our dogs to also have a different experience for ten days. I think she is right that a variation in our dogs' routine is a good thing.

I felt excitement to be with my family, anticipation and

hesitation to be there without Maddie, and some minor scary thoughts about giving up my everyday life, which includes Miss Betty.

Life is life, and it is a crazy ride—some good, some bad, and some unspeakable tragedies. You must keep your perspective. Remember: the ride is pretty short, and you must endure what the world has in store for you. I am so much luckier than most, and I know and appreciate that even when life makes each breath difficult, nothing is guaranteed. I appreciate that I can give my family this five-year gift we all cherish, with memories of all our time in this world.

Chapter 12

BACK FROM HAWAII

On the morning we left for Hawaii, we had to get up at 5:30 a.m. to get to the airport and catch our plane. We were very busy with last-minute items, but throughout all this organized chaos, I was focused on Miss Betty. Our dog sitter was there with her dog, Whiskey. Uncle Frank was close by, but Miss Betty was underneath and constantly by my feet. She was saying, "Hey! What's going on? What's happening? Why is the dog sitter here?"

Miss Betty knew we were leaving, and she did not want us to go. I had totally mixed feelings. I wanted to spend time with my family in Hawaii, but I didn't want to leave Miss Betty and Uncle Frank.

But we did. We left for the airport and left Miss Betty behind.

Over the next few hours, we were busy going through the TSA lines, checking our luggage, getting to our seats, and making our connecting flight in San Francisco.

Once in Hawaii, we got our luggage, picked up a rental car, and made the hour-long drive to our hotel.

Whew!

The ten-day family reunion was magical, and all thirteen of us got to interact with each other, eat together, and snorkel together. We went to a luau together and even had private time and one-on-one time. Our grandson Jacob could not make the trip, because he and his wife, Abbie, were about to become parents for the first time. On the last day of our trip, June 17, 2022, Michael was born, and we all became aunts, uncles, grandparents, and for Jenny and I, great-grandparents. A very big honor for us all.

We hated leaving one another, but our lives were calling.

We buckled down and took the twelve-hour trip home, with delayed planes, layovers, and the drive home. We got to our house around one o'clock in the morning.

I opened the door and spent the next ten minutes just loving Miss Betty, who was crying helplessly, and Uncle Frank.

What a great reunion for us all. Miss Betty did not leave my side for three full days, until she was sure I was not leaving her again. Even going to the grocery store was a bit traumatic for Miss Betty. When I returned within the hour, she was reassured but still stayed close to me.

After four days, things went back to normal, and Miss Betty was happy. I talked to her a lot, and we caught up on things like taking walks, napping, and getting food made with love.

The reception we get when we return is wonderful for all of us. Miss Betty is wild with jumps, licks, and pure happiness. I am full of joy at seeing my best friends: Miss Betty and Uncle Frank. I, too, jump around with pure joy, but no licking. I am not a big fan of licks, but I know Miss Betty must give me a couple of big licks. I limit it to just a few.

She slept next to me as I watched TV and curled into a ball right by my side, letting me know she was where she wanted to be and where she needed to be.

We are both happy, and that is what life is all about—small but precious moments that are burned into our memories forever. A small touch; a hand resting on her side; the knowledge that this is our moment, our time, our life. We are happy to be in the moment. Happy to share a touch, a heartbeat, a love.

Chapter 13

TRAUMATIC TIMES

Miss Betty went to the groomers one morning, and it was a traumatic event.

We got up early, and it was a morning like any other. Miss Betty was following me around, and we went outside to greet the day and to sit on the patio furniture and enjoy the cool air, which we knew would turn very warm in the afternoon. Into the high nineties was expected, so we enjoyed a cool start to the day. I got Miss Betty's leash, which always excites her, and told her that she was going to go with Dad that morning. I told Uncle Frank he was not going, but we would be back shortly. Uncle Frank understood and went to his soft, comfortable dog bed to await our return. Miss Betty, however, was a bit confused that Uncle Frank was not going, but she went right for the car, and I gently put her in the front seat.

As soon as we started moving, poor Miss Betty began to shake. "It's OK, Miss Betty," I reassured her. "We are just going to get you washed and groomed."

She didn't care; she was nervous. I talked to her and tried to rub her softly to let her know everything was going to be OK.

No amount of talking was going to work. Was it because we were in a car? We have been in the car many times in the past. Was it because Uncle Frank was not going too? I didn't think so.

I tried to make the best of it. Off we went to the groomers, about twenty-five minutes from home.

When we got there, Miss Betty was anxious to get out of the car. Before we walked inside, I gave her a big hug and hoped to reassure her.

Out of the car we went into Just Dog Pet Grooming. We were greeted, and Miss Betty was comfortable. The groomer, Carolyn, was charming and liked Miss Betty, and the receptionist, Matthew, was just as enthusiastic to see Miss Betty. She was groomed every five weeks, and this was her eighth visit since we moved to Reno, Nevada.

In went our raggedy dog, and I was told to pick her up in two hours.

I was worried, but she was in good hands. It felt like leaving my young children to go to kindergarten when they were very young many years ago.

I ran some errands while she was "in the shop."

Two hours later, I went to pick up Miss Betty, and she was beautiful. The groomer had done her magic, and my little, shaggy dog was now an adorable puppy with a clean face and well-groomed body. She had a little sparkle in her step, and she was so glad to see me. A momentary love fest ensued.

As soon as she got in the car and was buckled in the passenger seat, she didn't start shaking.

Was it because she felt beautiful? Was it the subtle smell of soap? I didn't know, but Miss Betty was a different dog in looks and attitude.

When we finished our twenty-five-minute ride home, Miss Betty was raring to get out and see Uncle Frank—to show off, I'm sure.

Was this something all women had over men? *Hey, look at me. I'm beautiful. Hey, look . . .* Uncle Frank does not display this "sparkle" when he gets groomed. Or was Miss Betty *feeling it?*

Uncle Frank was thrilled to see her, and they ran around each other. They sped through the front yard. She ran inside first and headed straight for the water bowl. Miss Betty took a long, cool drink, then let me know she was ready to go out back to show off to all the lizards, butterflies, and whatever else was out back. The mom and dad quails with their sixteen little babies that looked like small dust balls were not impressed and headed for the cover of a thick shrub.

Miss Betty didn't mind; she felt pretty and was telling all who would listen. Soon she came inside and sat beside me. Instantly, she relaxed and fell asleep. What a traumatic start to the day, and what a wonderful return. Sound asleep and comfortable in a space she belonged. Everything was good.

And mind you, this was not even noon yet.

Soon she would wake up and walk around the house, showing off her new grooming.

What a fun day, and the afternoon was just beginning.

We all need the opportunity to dress up, clean up, and feel special. We need that sparkle in our step. We need to be noticed, if even in the most modest way. We all need to strut our stuff once in a while. We need to forget all our work, schedules, stress, and daily worries. We need to take some time out to "sparkle."

We will return soon enough to real life, but just for a moment we need to get out of our comfort zones. We need to do this multiple times a year. Maybe this story will remind you to "be kind to yourself, love yourself, and get a grooming."

It sure helped Miss Betty. Even though she started out shaking, she ended up strutting.

Chapter 14

TRUST

I think trust is important between Miss Betty and myself. Trust is integrity and the ability to have faith in someone. With Miss Betty, I have instilled this trust between us. She trusts me because she can rely on me and the things I do. I don't take our trust lightly.

We have a pond in our backyard with three waterfalls, which is a delight to have. Miss Betty loves the pond but only goes in the first step by herself, a depth of about eight inches. When I go into the pond, which is about four and a half feet deep, I call to her, but she resists going in. I have a life jacket for her, but mentally that does not help. She will, with a lot of persuasion, come to me and let me take her in my arms, and I will walk around the pond, holding her. She trusts me not to let go. She gets back on land and races around the pond, in and out of the waterfalls. There is our trust, and it's building.

She knows I'm trustworthy. This helps in major ways all the time. If I tell her to come, she does not hesitate. If we are out walking on our trails, sometimes I need to keep her close when she is off-leash. We have coyotes in our area, and there are too many stories of small dogs being taken, even when the owner is present. While on our walks, I keep my eyes on the grass around us. If I feel even a little nervous, I call Miss Betty to get closer to me. And she does.

When I am in the yard, Miss Betty is always nearby. Doing yard work does not impress her, and often she will lay down in the shade while keeping an eye on me, but offering no help. A supervisor position, I'm guessing, though I have no idea who promoted her.

When I hand-water the plants, she takes notice and will come up to me, knowing I will lower the hose so she can take a drink. I do not splash her; I do not tease her, as a lot of people do. Even though it's hot, I don't splash her. This is where the trust comes in again. If she needs a drink, she will come up to me, and I'll let her have a drink. If I'm watering a plant close to where she is laying, she knows I will not splash her. She does not move, even when the water is inches from her.

I like that we have this trust.

If I need to give her some medicine that the doctor ordered, she lets me without any fight or resistance.

She is a dog. But not to me. She is a family member and is treated as such. To her, I am her entire world. Jenny and Uncle Frank are also very important to her, but I am her best buddy—especially in the afternoons, when the day is starting to catch up with her, and a soft, comfortable, trustworthy person is all she wants. And here I am.

I think we all need that one fully trustworthy person who is your true friend—your comfort zone. Where you will not be splashed, where you can let go in the deep pond, and where a drink of water is always available to you without fear. Trust is a very important part of our world. I love looking into Miss Betty's brown eyes, knowing I will not let her down. Ever.

Chapter 15

OUR TIME TOGETHER

Miss Betty is not going to last forever, but nothing does.

I'm certainly not going to last forever, and at seventy-three my life has a termination date in the near future. I don't think I will last another twenty years, but I have always thought I will live to see ninety-three.

I don't dwell on such things. I have always had the ability to live "in the moment." I think about the future as far as planning and the economics of what it will take to live comfortably.

But I live in the now. I appreciate all I have; I do not dream of more and more, as some people do. My house is sufficient, and I do not need or want a mansion. The same can be said of my car, my food, and my lifestyle.

I'm OK where I am and don't fill my head with dreams of living someplace else.

I have always enjoyed my life. When things got tough, I knew they would pass because I wanted and worked hard at making tough times leave me alone.

I am living my life in the early twenty-first century and enjoy the world I am in. Sure, artificial intelligence is just around the corner, and I suppose pretty soon the world will have artificial life to help us in our daily chores. But that's not now.

As I write this, I am in a comfortable room with my special trinkets around me, but more importantly, I have Uncle Frank and Miss Betty laying by my feet, enjoying the life we have all made possible.

Miss Betty is lightly sleeping and ready to wake at any moment if I move even an inch. She is ready for any adventure that may arise. We took a long walk just an hour ago, so she is resting after our exercise. She loves our daily walks, as does Uncle Frank, but the weather has been in the high nineties, so I spray them off before we walk, then we walk on a dirt path so their feet do not get too hot. If I see them begin to show signs of getting too hot, we simply turn around and head home. It is a good system, and both dogs are up for a walk at any time.

Miss Betty and I are enjoying our life. We do not long for anything. We get up each morning, raring to go, and most days we have no specific direction. We go out and greet the morning, walk around the yard, and see what's going on. We check the morning news, stock market, and emails. Then coffee, for me, and we walk the front and back yards.

It's a great life. I'm long retired, and Miss Betty is up for anything.

When I write, Miss Betty relaxes by my feet. I often share my thoughts and work with her, but she does not seem to care. I know she must like what I am typing because she never discourages me from writing. Yes, our time together will end.

But that is an issue for another day. I may go first, and I know

Miss Betty will really miss me and will keep looking for me. Or she may go first, and I will be a wreck. There will never be another Miss Betty. I got the original, and she cannot be duplicated. I am lucky to have her in my life at this very moment. I appreciate her and will never let her feel unloved as long as I am here.

But we are not meant to be here for a long time. Life has a way of going pretty quickly, and for those who don't appreciate that, I feel sorry for you. Every minute I am alive, I look around and marvel at the wonderful life we have been given.

I love the colors of every dusk, when the sky puts on a show of pinks, oranges, and grays as the day's sun leaves us until tomorrow. I breathe the fresh air that we are fortunate to have, and I take in the cool, clean water that nature provides. I love the wonderful smell of cooked meals and the delicious taste of fresh fruit.

These are things we are blessed to have and to enjoy. All we have to do is take a moment to reflect on the good things that surround us. Miss Betty is in that wonderment. A beautiful little dog that we are blessed to have in our life. A little girl that needs food, water, and love, with love being the thing that gives her comfort and lets her know her life is good.

We don't last forever, and that is OK. In hard times and in good times, we must look at each other and say, "This is the life I was given and the time I was given to live in. May I be blessed and bless all those in my circle of life."

Time continues and does not stop for anyone or anything. It is important to appreciate life—that wonderful thing we are a part of for only a few short years.

Love where you are, love who you are with, love this time in your life. It is all we have.

Chapter 16

COMPANION

I tend to be pretty healthy, but not because I spend hours and hours exercising and eating only the right foods. It's because I learned long ago to do everything in moderation. That and I have good genes.

I don't overeat, and I don't eat lots of bad or fast food. I love sugar, I enjoy a cold Pepsi, and I enjoy fast food, but not all the time. I eat these things in moderation. I don't overtax my body.

Most of the time, when family members or friends are committed to lots of exercise or what they consider "eating right," I have found that these tend to be passing fads. They are gung ho for a period of time, but before long they give up and end up where I am—in moderation.

That being said, I do get migraines, which is a headache, blurred vision, and a feeling of nausea. Something that knocks me down, not literally, but I am out of commission.

When I was working in a high-pressure job, I would get a migraine every five to six weeks. They were the result of pressure, not eating consistently, and caffeine. I gave up caffeinated coffee, Pepsi, and tried to take a few moments for myself. Work was all-consuming, and my lunch was never guaranteed— stress was guaranteed.

When I retired, all the stress just fell off my shoulders, and life was more stress-free. But as we all know, life has its stressors at every level. Even retired, I got the occasional migraine. I experience them to this day.

I woke up yesterday and felt fine, but two hours into the day I got a migraine. My vision was blurred, I felt nauseated, and I had a headache. This happens very quickly. I go from being fine to being so sick that I have to lay down in a dark space.

I woke up, and Miss Betty was ready for an exciting day. But all of a sudden, I was back in bed, fully clothed. This seemed to confuse Miss Betty. Nevertheless, she quickly climbed up close to me and stayed quiet and calm. I could feel her there, but I was unable to pet her or even talk to her. I was combating the migraine monster that inhabits me from time to time.

I have migraine medicine that I take just as soon as I feel the migraine, but it never seems to help much.

With Miss Betty snuggled up close to me, I sleep but constantly toss and turn, trying to get comfortable. Miss Betty allows me to move as much as I need, then she adjusts and goes to sleep too.

After about six hours, I begin to move and try getting up. I hate to waste a day, but I am sick, so back to sleep I go. Miss Betty stays with me, protecting me and comforting me and being my companion. She does not complain that she might have to go to the bathroom; she does not let me know she might be hungry. She stays with me without complaint.

The migraine comes quickly and without warning, but she

goes away slowly, and for the next two days I am still nauseated, not hungry, and generally off.

Miss Betty sees this and is nothing but a friend during these times. She demands nothing from me and only wants to comfort me. During the next few days, when I sit in a chair and semisleep or just sit there enjoying the view down the hill into the town of Reno, Nevada, Miss Betty never wavers. Miss Betty sits on my lap or sits beside me and sleeps when I do. She is also awake when I am.

Such a good companion.

I have a wife who checks on me occasionally, but even she knows Miss Betty is the constant in my migraine hell. She knows Miss Betty will not leave me alone and will stand guard for as long as it takes.

I do get better within a few days, and I let Miss Betty know that I love her and appreciate all the time she has put into getting me back to good health.

It is this reason that I take Miss Betty for walks, even when I do not want to go. I owe her for all the love I receive.

Dogs are funny creatures. As soon as you get one, they instantly become family. If you have dedicated yourself to owning a dog, you know what I'm talking about. Miss Betty is not just a dog; she is *Miss Betty*—my friend, companion, and someone I love. I will protect her, treat her with kindness, and dedicate myself to her as she has done to me.

We should all be so lucky as to have someone in our life who loves us without question. Someone who is there for us, who loves to see us, and who makes us feel special. We need to return that favor and love and protect that one. Miss Betty is special to me, and you have someone special to you if you have a dog.

Chapter 17

SICK

Miss Betty is healthy and happy, but the other morning when we got out of bed to start our day, I noticed Miss Betty was not moving with her usual zest. She was laying on her side and looked like a little rag dog. I went over to her and gave her a pet and encouraged her to get up. She just looked at me with her big brown eyes, and I knew she was not feeling well.

I felt like one of my children was sick. I instantly knew our day had just changed from one of a busy schedule to waiting on Miss Betty. She was the priority for the day and as long as it took to get her back to feeling good.

Whenever I had a migraine, Miss Betty would be there for me. It was now my turn to be there for her.

I did an assessment and discovered all her get-up-and-go was gone. I rubbed her head softly because I know she loves that. It made her close her eyes. She went back to sleep. This little dog on our big, king-size bed. So cute and so sad all at the same time.

I called the veterinarian and talked to the doctor. Her

suggestion was to wait it out. Let Miss Betty sleep as long as she could, then give her water and just a small amount of dry food. If things did not get better, or if she got worse, then rush her in. The doctor was optimistic Miss Betty had a one-day sickness and was confident this healthy dog would be fine by later in the day or tomorrow.

I was now the nurse for Miss Betty, lying beside her, watching her sleep. It was so peaceful in the bedroom, with the morning sun warming us up, that I drifted off as I laid beside her. When I woke up, I was looking into her eyes as she stared at me. What a cute dog I have.

She seemed to feel better but was reluctant to sit up or leave the bed. I just laid beside her and talked to her, telling her about the first time I met her at the breeder's. I know she understood little of what I was telling her, but I felt good reliving the special first time I met her. She was so tiny that she fit in the palm of my hand. Now she was a healthy, twenty-pound dog. Well, not completely healthy, but we were working on that.

When she did feel better, she walked with me into the kitchen and drank a little water and a bit of food but with no gusto. I took her and put her on the couch beside me with a warm soft blanket below her and around her sides. She was comfortable and slowly went back to sleep. I read my latest book while she slept. I needed to be near her—to be there for her, to watch her recover. After many chapters, she woke up, but now with a twinkle in her eye. I took her outside, and she instantly went to the lawn to go to the bathroom, then began roaming the backyard, looking at all the boulders to find a lizard or two.

Miss Betty was back. She walked with confidence, she looked right and left, and she experienced the yard she loved, with its various plant life and tree cover.

She was Miss Betty again.

We all need someone to look after us when we don't feel well or have a problem that needs looking after. It may be sickness or a rough patch in life. We need each other. It is important to be the one helping when we can. Be that friend, that soft spot, that helping hand. It is nice to help and be helped. We are a community, a family, humanity.

Chapter 18

COMMUNICATION

Miss Betty does not talk. She does not have to. She communicates with me just fine. When I ask her if she is hungry around five, which is dinnertime, she licks her lips, and that tells me to fix her dinner. If I ask her, and she does not lick her lips, I know she is not ready to eat, and I wait a while to feed her.

This is just one of the many ways we have learned to communicate with each other. The communication takes place all day long and throughout the night.

If we are all done with dinner and sitting around watching TV, I hear Miss Betty squeak to let me know she needs to go out. If I am not fast enough or don't really hear her, or even ignore her, she moves a chair in the breakfast area. To hear a chair moving is disturbing, to say the least, but Miss Betty is making a point. *I have to go potty now!* I get up and open the door for her, and out she goes.

When she does this, I call her the Boss. I don't think it's natural for a dog to be moving furniture around to get her point across.

But Miss Betty is special, and I love that she has come up with a unique form of communication.

She does have a cry that has several meanings.

She will cry when she wants the food I am eating, but I almost never give her my food while I eat. That is an easy thing to do but creates a bad habit that is hard to break; however, it is communication, and that's an important part of our relationship.

I take Miss Betty out for a walk every day, and she knows this. If she thinks I am being lazy or negligent, she comes looking for me and has a nonstop whine that only increases if I say, "Want to go for a walk?"

After dinner she has a burst of energy, and I often ask Jenny, "Did you just replace her batteries?" which I think is funny. Jenny? Not so much anymore. Miss Betty runs at maximum speed all around the house and loves it when I chase her or hide behind a door or wall to jump out at her. Lord, what fun! She will run for ten minutes without stopping.

Then Miss Betty winds down, and before long she is sitting right next to me with drowsy eyes. Soon she is curled up and asleep next to me while I caress her softly.

This is a great part of our communication, when she knows she is safe and gently snores in a deep sleep.

But is it really a deep sleep? It looks like it, and she does not wake up easily, except when at the end of the evening I say, "Who wants to go to bed?" She is up like lightning and runs to the front door as I let her out to go potty before bed. She rushes back in and heads straight to bed.

She pretends to sleep while I get ready for bed, then curls up next to me and goes to sleep for the night.

Throughout the day, Miss Betty talks to me in a language that only she and I recognize—a look here; a whine there; a scratch on my leg; or her special, when she steps on my heel as I'm walking to get my attention.

Sometimes I look at her and say, "You looking at me? You want a piece of this? You sure?" I chase her, and I can almost hear her laughing.

Outdoors, when she is off-leash, which is not too often, I will call her in a firm voice that means, "Come here now."

I need her to know when I am not kidding, and I am serious. When she does, I give her a lot of praise.

Dogs are fun and have distinct personalities, just like people. Miss Betty is a hoot and a lot of fun. I'm glad we have our communication.

We all have nonverbal communications with those close to us—a look, a smile, a wink, a shrug. We have special communication with words that others often do not get. But we all communicate with each other each day. Communication is important between humans and our pets. Talking and caressing are all important parts of interactions.

I hope you all have special ways to "talk" during the day. I do, and I love that I have special meanings with my loved ones.

Chapter 19

LAKE TAHOE

We live forty-five minutes from Lake Tahoe, a large, beautiful, clear, clean lake high in the Sierra Nevada. We have a condominium in Incline Village, a small town on the north side of the lake. We often go up to the lake for a week or whenever we feel like getting away. Miss Betty loves going to the lake. She knows we will be able to take a walk along the trails and creeks going into the lake, and she knows she is allowed to go into the creeks—to splash around and get totally wet and dirty.

We walk slowly together along the meandering path that intersects with the creek. Miss Betty refuses to use the bridges and goes directly into the creek to cross. I laugh as she negotiates the cold water. Back up the bank and on the path with me, she shakes to get the water off. We continue our journey and come to the "heart rock," which is easily seen but only if one knows where to look. We say hi to the rock every time we pass.

Off we go to the large, open grass field, where all the dogs congregate and run and run. When we come up to the field, a group of dogs stop what they are doing and come greet Miss Betty. She is thrilled but keeps an eye on me to be sure this is OK. She enthusiastically trades sniffs with the other dogs. A big festival of dogs all greeting Miss Betty, until a new dog approaches, and now Miss Betty is with the welcoming committee. We stay for a while, then all the dogs slowly meander away to their owners and other interests.

I take Miss Betty home slowly and stop at our porch so I can hose her off and get rid of all the dirt and grime. I dry her off in the warm sun. She is very happy. We go inside our home, and Miss Betty relaxes in front of the fireplace. Tired from all the exertion, she curls up and is fast asleep. I'm pretty sure she is dreaming of all the fun we had today and all the adventures tomorrow will bring.

It is always fun to do something different yet familiar. Miss Betty loves the adventures that await her at Lake Tahoe. Getting away is a special time and always creates memories. Memories of life are to be acquired and used whenever you need to daydream.

Chapter 20

FAMILY

What is family? Is it the people we grew up with? Our mom and dad? Our brothers and sisters? Aunts, uncles, and cousins?

Yes, it is all of that, but what about the people you meet along the road of life? People you are close with in school—are they family?

College seems to bind people who have similar interests and career paths.

How do you define *family* when it goes beyond blood relation?

My definition includes people who support each other, provide a sense of security, and have an unconditional love for each other. All this clearly comes into focus when we have a disaster in our life or a serious tragedy, when family comes together to offer love, understanding, and support.

I met a woman who had parents and four brothers. She was thirty-five when I met her, and she was the middle child. I did not know her family, as they were all grown and matured. They married and had children. I knew nothing of this. Within a couple of years, we were married, and they became my "family." But being "family" takes time and effort, for the most part. Interactions and the acquisition of memories are slowly developed over time. It has been thirty-three years now, and we are fully family.

My aunts and uncles have slowly passed away, as well as a few cousins, which is terribly sad for me. But as my childhood family began to diminish, my adult family began to expand.

I have been fortunate in my life because I am part of a large family. I love all my family, and as it expands, I have begun to lose sight of some of my cousins' children's children. But that is OK because I have a core family that makes me comfortable. We have had family reunions, and although I don't know them all, we are a part of a living, breathing group who share a common bond.

Sometimes we choose our family.

I have friends who have become family over the years. They are invited to holidays and important dates in each other's lives. Rick, Robert, and Rob, their wives, and children are a part of my family. That is how I see them and how we see each other.

Which brings me to Miss Betty.

She was just a puppy in a litter of twelve puppies that we seemed to have a bond with, along with another puppy. The other puppy had some cute markings, but Miss Betty sold me with her soft, sweet eyes that seemed to be saying a lot. Eyes that said, "I'm here. I will *love* you forever, and I am a great choice for you."

I understood her, and the rest is history. Miss Betty is family. She is treated with respect and loved as a member of our family. She was chosen to be a part of our family.

She has a special place in our family because she will live her entire life with us.

We have four children who we have raised to be self-sufficient, contributing citizens. Three are married, with children of their own. We even have two great-grandchildren. We raised them, they spread their wings, and we were proud to see them soar off into the world.

We love each of them, and we are a very close family, but they no longer live with us. Miss Betty and Uncle Frank do and will for as long as they live. We know this, and we are their support. It is our duty to care for these wonderful dogs with good food, clean water, long walks, and a restful, warm night's sleep. We take them to the veterinarian when they need to go. We provide good, balanced food and a safe environment. We have committed to these family members, and we will uphold our commitment. That is family.

When our family gets together at our house, our children, their spouses, and their children all rush to Miss Betty and Uncle Frank, as they, too, are family. Miss Betty and Uncle Frank reciprocate with love, and it is a wonderful thing to see our family together. Family is important.

This is the family both Miss Betty and Uncle Frank know. They interact with all the family and are so excited when they come here.

We all talk family, but an effort is required to make it all work. You need to touch base—to communicate with one another to keep family together. We speak about family a lot in America, but we do not always see the warmth and love that family generates. If you are a part of a family, please make an effort to communicate with each other. A true family goes through good times and tough times together. Call each other, even if occasionally, to keep the bond fresh.

Chapter 21

WINTER

Winter has come to Reno, Nevada. That means snow—beautiful, cold snow. Miss Betty and I are from California, and we are used to a mild winter. We lived in Carmel, California, which has a beautiful climate all year long. It is a coastal resort town and is known for its year-round mild temperatures. The weather changes little from summer to winter, and not at all from spring to fall. Miss Betty is unsure of snow, even though this is her second year experiencing the cold white fluff. Carefully, she goes outside, but then stops to assess her surroundings. She tiptoes into the snow, then must remember what a fun time snow is as she blasts around the courtyard, going from right to left, top to bottom, and everywhere in between.

For a full ten minutes, she is having the time of her life; then she must get cold, because she wants to come inside. "Hold on, Miss Betty. You are covered in small, hard, white snowballs from head to toe." I get the large beach towel that we put by every door at the first sign of winter just for this reason. I also grab the whisk. Yes, the same one you use to whisk gravy. It is a wonderful tool to get most of the snowballs off Miss Betty in a quick, efficient manner without any complaints from Miss Betty.

We dry her off, then put on her winter sweater, which she loves. Soon she is cuddled up and sound asleep.

The funny thing is, the snow sticks to Miss Betty when it is fresh, but if we get a few days without any new snow, the snow that is already in the yard does not stick to her fur. I find that interesting.

In the backyard, whether it is snowing or just a backyard with a few inches of snow, when I let out Miss Betty and Uncle Frank, they just run and run after each other. Miss Betty is the boss and chases Uncle Frank; then Uncle Frank is the boss and chases Miss Betty. They run in big circles, and they run the entire yard. We have two and a half acres, but we have fenced off about an acre in the backyard, and the dogs run and run throughout that space. It always makes me giggle. They are having *so* much fun. When they stop for a break, they each dive into the snow and cover themselves up with snow. Just the top of their brown backs contrasting with the white snow. They lay there for a moment, quickly get up, shake themselves off, then search for each other to continue the game. What fun!

I love to see my dogs have so much fun. When my children were growing up, I held the same amazement and had the same giggles to see them have so much fun. These are the days we all remember. Fun-filled, running in circles, swimming in the pool, enjoying the summer sun on your back. Being a family, being safe, and being able to act silly.

Good memories. Uncle Frank and Miss Betty give me those giggles each day. It is something I cherish now, as the end of my time is somewhere in the future. How far in the future? I do not know, but at seventy-three, I know it is coming. I do not worry, and I do not fear the end.

What I do is enjoy each and every day. I look at Miss Betty, and I laugh at all the times we are enjoying.

We are enjoying the snow from this winter and do not think about how many winters we have left. This winter is plenty enough for us. We still have spring to look forward to—then summer, fall, winter, spring, and so on. We enjoy each moment, each day, each meal, and each evening. When we sleep to rejuvenate our bodies, we wake up full of anticipation for the wonders of the day to unfold before us.

We look forward to the afternoon we will share—afternoons with Miss Betty.

Winter lets us know the seasons are passing. We don't try to hurry these things up. They go at a pace we can enjoy—a pace that allows us to feel the snowflakes, see the spring flowers, feel the summer heat, and watch the fall colors. Each season is interesting and a bit different; each day has its own challenges and wonders. This is a wonderful life, and I enjoy each afternoon with Miss Betty, my friend and buddy.

We should all have an opportunity to enjoy what life has to offer. Many of us are hard at work, raising our families, making money to survive, and we all have some heartache, but I hope you can all get to where I am with Miss Betty. I wish you luck and an attitude to succeed.

Chapter 22

LOVES ME

Miss Betty loves me and likes my wife, and that is OK. It's fine to favor one over the other. I think we all do that all day long with our family and friends. We choose to like one better than another. We love them all but tend to favor some a bit more.

Is it because they relate more, and we have more in common with them? I don't know, but I do know it is a fact of life.

With Miss Betty, it is because I spend more time with her. I am the one who walks her and the one who feeds her. She sleeps on my side of the bed each night, snuggled up to my legs, fast asleep and safe.

My wife does walk her and feed her, but only occasionally, when I am gone or out of town. I am the one who is consistent in her life.

I think that is an important factor in a strong relationship— to be able to depend on someone who is close to you. My children know they can always count on me for advice, for a favor, for an opinion, for support.

Family are close, and you can count on them because you grew up together, but friends are people you turn to when you have similar opinions about issues. Some friends are in agreement most of the time, and some friends are the ones you want to talk to if you have different opinions.

I disagree with some of my friends about politics. I have two options when I am with them: discuss the issues and be open to hearing what the other has to say, or stay quiet on the entire subject. Know that you are going to disagree, so keep it out of the discussion. I have lost friends because of political disagreements. We just don't agree, and yet we can't talk without bringing up politics.

People are just more comfortable with some than others. I don't have a lot of close friends, but the ones I have are longtime, true friends who can discuss any subject or issue.

It turns out, we are closest to those who we know will be there for us, who do not ridicule us, and who we feel safe in discussions.

The same is true for Miss Betty. She knows I will be there for her. I will have her best interest in mind, and anything I do for her is to help her.

It is important for Miss Betty to feel safe and loved in our family. Whenever family or friends stop by, they all always give Miss Betty a big hello and lots of head rubs. She runs in circles and is terribly excited and has to greet everyone before she settles down.

I love that my family and friends love Miss Betty, and I love that Miss Betty is a social part of our lives.

We all need security and comfort. Not all of us are that lucky to have these comforts. It is something to cherish if you have a circle around you who gives you comfort.

Chapter 23

DRESSING UP MISS BETTY

As I have said throughout this book, Miss Betty is a cute and petite little dog. Well! My wife thought it would be fun to put Miss Betty in a dress. "Oh no! That is a terrible idea," I moaned as my wife pulled a dress from the Amazon package that just arrived.

"Oh! What fun!" she exclaimed as I withered in the corner.

"What are you doing to my little Miss Betty?" But Miss Betty got a dress that fit surprisingly well. And Miss Betty looked so cute that I had to laugh and say out loud, "She looks wonderful. Good job on getting her a dress, honey."

The dress was a Scottish plaid dress with two brass buttons on her back. It changed her look and attitude. She got so many compliments that she was prancing around, showing off her new wardrobe. And I liked it—hard to believe. I have always said a man should be in a relationship with a woman because they both think so differently, and that complements the relationship. I would have *never* put a dress on Miss Betty, but now that she has one on, it is so unique.

But my wife went too far, because she bought some clothes for Uncle Frank, our forty-pound dog, and Uncle Frank said a rousing, "No way!" and ran from my wife. There was no way Uncle Frank was going to "get dressed," and I had to laugh at that.

My wife, thinking she did a good thing with Miss Betty, bought four more dresses that she pulled out every so often. Soon I was seeing Miss Betty in new outfits about every week. Some were cute, and some were not. The Scottish outfit could not be beat, but my wife was certainly trying.

I did have to take off her outfits so her beautiful fur could get some fresh air, and I could just pet her when she sat next to me. It has been a while now, and I am used to seeing Miss Betty walk around with her dresses on. I am no longer shocked to see this spectacle. I do take the dresses off when we go for a walk. It just does not seem appropriate to have a dog with a dress and a leash, *and* I don't want people to see me with a prissy, little foo-foo dog. It challenges my manhood. Often on a walk, when I pass someone, they comment on my cute little dog, but I can only imagine what they might say if she were sporting a little dress. "Uh, OK, uh, nice dress, Mister." No thanks, that's not the type of comment I want. It does add some charm to Miss Betty, and while she is in this house or in the yard, I am content to have her dressed up. I'm just not so sure as to leave the house with her dressed up. And that's all I'm going to say about that. Period.

We all need to be pushed to try different things out of our comfort zone. We need to taste life, and we cannot do that if we don't reach out, try something new, explore, and at least try. New experiences are important and add to the texture of life. We should all try things from the North, South, East, West, above, below, and within.

Chapter 24

INDEPENDENCE

Miss Betty is now three years old and is a firm member of our family. She has learned our daily routine—the hours we are awake, when we eat, when we go for walks, when we go to sleep, and all the intricacies of our life. We run on a routine but not time. Miss Betty has an instinct about routine and knows when we need to do things, such as take a nap or eat food.

I don't wear a watch for all these moments we have during a typical day.

I learned a long time ago that I do not want to have a watch on my wrist. I can always find the time of day. I figured that when I was in a meeting or just talking with a friend, that was my sole focus. I would take whatever time necessary to enjoy that moment. Having a watch made me look at it often to check the time. Did it really matter? No, not most of the time. I enjoyed the time I was spending with someone without time limits. Miss Betty and I rely on a routine, but it's not based on a specific time.

Now that I'm retired, that is an even better philosophy. If I am eating lunch, I take my time to enjoy the meal. Each bite is enhanced, the scenery is appreciated, and the time does not matter. It is a good way to live. It makes life more meaningful.

My point is, life for us does have a time routine and is not dictated by a watch.

Miss Betty knows this, and she has started to become more independent. When she thinks it's time for a snack, she will come up to me and let it be known with a small whine that she is ready for a little something to eat.

I have a sweater I put on her during the cold winter days. I take it off at times when I think she is too warm. If later on she is chilly, she will come up to me and let me know she wants her sweater back on. She stands close to the sweater, paws it, and gives her little whine. And I put her sweater back on.

She also lets me know when she needs to go out in the yard and when she is tired and ready to nap or go to bed.

She is now an independent lady who lets me know what she likes and when she likes it. It is fun to see Miss Betty mature and communicate with me. Time is such a funny concept. It is important, and it is not important.

During your working career, time is very important. And raising a family runs on a schedule. But once you get used to time being only a way to count things, you will find that time can be adjusted. Things that are important can be given more time.

You only get one shot at this life, and it is important to use your time wisely. It is the only thing you cannot get more of.

I have learned to appreciate time and to use it wisely without being a slave to the clock. I enjoy my days and fit in as much as I can without looking at a clock. The sun lets me know where I am in the day.

I saw a funny clock that had no hours on it. It only had the days of the week. There was a marking to show when half the day was gone. You would look at that clock and say, "It's Wednesday in the afternoon. I might want to get something done today." No concept of the hour, only that it was Wednesday afternoon.

Miss Betty knows this better than anyone.

Chapter 25

REASON

I have written a lot about Miss Betty and our relationship, but I want to address the "reason" we have Miss Betty.

This is hard for me to write about, but it is my life and what was given to me—my hardship.

Let me start at the beginning.

I have four amazing children—three beautiful daughters and a handsome son. They are all adults and are wonderful people. They are interesting, fun to be around, and they are working to make this world better.

As young children, they were so much fun and taught me so much about being a dad. Those were busy days, with work, children, and all that entails being a family. They now are in those busy times of life, and I am retired. To those who are retired, know that you are never fully retired from life—from a job, yes, but not from life. You are always a dad, and your children are always your children. They grow up and have their own families, but they are still your family.

I loved the kids being young and learning. I loved the stage where they began to "come into their own," and I loved the time when they "got their wings" and began to fly all on their own.

All you want for your children is to be happy, healthy, and to enjoy life and experience all that life has to offer.

My wife and I were excited about life, excited that our children were enjoying life, even though it was so busy for them.

Our youngest daughter had been living in Los Angeles for a few years to experience that lifestyle and was moving back up to the Bay Area to be closer to our family.

My wife and I were traveling back from a trip to Lake Tahoe on August 10, 2015, and our daughter was driving up from LA. We got a phone call from Madison, our youngest daughter. We had a five-minute talk with her and were laughing that both her and her mother had the same breakfast sandwich and latte that morning. She was so excited to start the next phase of her story, and we were excited that we were going to meet up with her at her new apartment and have dinner together. We got off the phone with "I love yous," and we looked at each other and said what a good kid she turned out to be.

We did not know it at the time, but within a couple of minutes of that call, Madison, age twenty-five, our youngest daughter, *was dead*. She was in a car accident and was instantly killed.

We waited for her at her new apartment. The movers were there, and our son had come over to help. We were moving in clothing and furniture. We began to call her, knowing if she had any car trouble she was smart enough to fix any situation.

Soon we began to panic, and I started to call Apple to see if they could trace her phone. My son began calling the Highway Patrol to see if there had been any accidents.

My son came up to me and said, "Put the phone down. Maddie has been in a single-car fatality."

I froze. I couldn't put the words together. I couldn't make sense of what I was hearing. *Single-car fatality? Fatality? She's dead? She's gone? My Maddie is dead?*

I ran to tell my wife. She was stunned. We could not talk. Our eyes went dead. Our world stopped.

I needed to go home. I needed to leave this place. I didn't know what to do. I was lost.

As I write this, it all comes rushing back.

My son said, "I'll drive you home."

"No," I said. "I think concentrating on driving will help me right now."

We took off for home. Within twenty minutes, I thought I was having a heart attack. My arms would not work. My wife said, "Pull over." She drove the rest of the way. My daughter always called me Baj. Now no one will call me Baj? We just talked to Maddie. She had a big personality. She couldn't be gone.

What? Wait. Maddie? I'm too upset to cry. No tears. Total confusion. What happened? What could have happened? Where was she? My wife was silent. No sounds. Just driving.

I moaned, but quietly. I was so confused.

The next few weeks were a blur. Not much eating—cereal, if anything. No good sleep. Burial plots, casket, plans, confusion. Thank God for our children. Krista and Holly worked tirelessly to put things together. My sister, Nancy, jumped into the fray to help anywhere. My son tried to help, but he was about to have a baby.

Life went dead. Sounds were muted. The world didn't matter.

Months passed, and we began to come out of our fog. We attended grief classes. We talked to counselors. Our forever-changed world was starting to open up to us. We still had children, grandchildren, friends, and family. They were all there for us.

Life does not stop. Life does not care if you have a setback. Life continues with or without you.

We tried to participate in the world, but we were not ready. We stuck around home—our safe haven.

As we began to open up, we decided a pet might be what we needed. New life, responsibility, and love. *This is where the story of Uncle Frank and Miss Betty starts.*

We got Uncle Frank, our wonderful labradoodle. He was some of the help we needed. He focused us; he needed us to participate in life. He needed food, sleep, and exercise. He made us live. As the years passed, and our new reality set in, we adjusted. We changed. We began living a new life.

Five years later, we decided to get another labradoodle, but a smaller dog. Soon Miss Betty was our responsibility. Another focus for us each day.

We will never be the same happy couple, but we are enjoying life. We love Uncle Frank and Miss Betty.

They are a welcome gift in our life, and we talk to them about Maddie. They know all our children. Maddie is someone we talk about so that her life, image, and story will never die in our lifetime.

This is how we got Miss Betty.

Thank you for being here, Miss Betty. Thank you.

Life is unpredictable, and we should all enjoy what we have. When something is taken from you, it puts everything else in perspective. We have four wonderful children. One is in heaven. She will have no wedding, no children, and no future, but she will always be remembered.

She is talked about all the time. We encourage it. She is at all our functions. It is a great burden to carry, but it is ours to carry. The sadness is always there. The loss is overwhelming.

A little dog with a big heart is a welcome relief for us.

Chapter 26

WE ALL NEED EACH OTHER

Miss Betty is my responsibility, and I took on that responsibility the day I thought about getting a dog—a cute little puppy that was eight weeks old and without a name or someone to commit to having her for life.

I took that pledge seriously and named her and gave her a warm home and a bed and a commitment to care for her for as long as she lives.

In turn, she has been an absolute joy and an important member of our family. We need her too. She also has a duty to me and my wife—to be friendly, endearing, a part of the daily routine. We need her as much as she needs us. We need her love, warmth, silliness, and seriousness.

When I think of it, we all need other people to help us, protect us, feed us, and house us.

I did not build our house. A team of professionals built this house based on architectural plans developed by another professional.

The wood for the house came from a tree that was processed by another team of people who know this profession.

The electricity came from a dam that was designed, built, and managed by another team of people. The windows, kitchen appliances, concrete—the list goes on and on.

I only eat because there are farmers dedicated to feeding America. The food is processed and ends up in a grocery store or farmers market for all of us to purchase.

The water we drink has been designed to be in our kitchen and bathrooms and outdoor faucets.

I sit on furniture and watch TV because people invented these comforts for us. The programming on TV is because people work hard every day to provide us with entertainment.

My car has a long history of design and development to provide me with transportation.

The clothes I wear every day consist of pants, shirts, shoes, and socks. Coats for cool weather and swimming attire for warm weather.

The fence I have in my yard to keep Miss Betty and Uncle Frank contained was created and installed by people who know fencing.

Miss Betty needs me, and I need a whole host of people who look out for me, house me, feed me, entertain me, and clothe me.

When we think this world owes us, we are mistaken. We owe this world everything.

Miss Betty and I are a team. We rely on each other every day. We make each other's world better.

I'm glad Miss Betty is in my life.

We all need people and animals in our lives. It enriches us. It gives life importance and meaning. We need to care for each other. Relationships are the texture of life. This silly, brown-eyed little dog is so important in my life. I'm glad we made the commitment to have another member of our family. We are indeed a lucky family.

Chapter 27

EATING

Feeding Miss Betty is the same as feeding a family, in that I have to mix it up each day. Miss Betty does not like to eat the same food day after day. It is my job to give her a balanced meal that she finds appetizing.

I give her a small bowl of kibble, with some freeze-dried kibble that she loves. That is for breakfast. She is hungry when she wakes up in the morning, so I feed her a simple meal. She eats it up and is satisfied for a long time.

In the afternoon, we take one or two walks. The weather sometimes dictates if we go or not, but 90 percent of the time we are good to go.

In the late afternoon, around five, I prepare her dinner.

This is a bigger meal, and during the winter months, I make her warm food.

I have hamburger-type meals for dogs that are beef or chicken or duck, etc. I add some fresh-cooked beef and vegetables made for dogs. On top of all this, I pour some chicken or beef bone broth, which they love.

This may sound like a lot of food, but it is not.

I feed Miss Betty a balanced meal and give her exercise each day to keep her at a trim twenty pounds.

When I take her to the vet, the first thing the doctor does is weigh Miss Betty, and it is a source of pride when her weight stays at a consistent twenty pounds.

I have to work on myself the same way, but sometimes my weight does not stay consistent. Darn it!

I try to exercise, but that is a lot of work. And not fun work, so I tend to slack off. I make myself believe that walking the dogs is exercise, but it is not. I need to burn more calories than the dogs. I try going to the gym, but I can easily talk myself out of it. I'm either too busy, too tired, or too lazy. There, I said it. Then I try to eat good, but that is not so simple.

Being retired, I no longer cook meals every day. I throw together salads and an occasional steak and spinach, but often I will buy a whole cooked chicken. The chicken feeds me and my wife, and there is plenty to feed the dogs for a few days. As a supplement to their meal, I occasionally give the dogs some chicken.

As I have gotten older, I find I really only need two meals a day. I get up and eat breakfast, which for me is Kashi cereal with cinnamon.

I eat the same thing every day, unless we go out to breakfast, which we do about twice a week. Then I am good until about three thirty, when I am hungry again. That is when I fix something from the house or go out and get a meal.

Because I eat restaurant-cooked meals, I think I get more butter and fat than if I cooked something at home. Restaurants cook for taste and flavor, and butter and fat are flavor. I just don't want to cook every day. Doing that for our whole working career and raising children was fine, and I really enjoyed family meals together. With just myself and my wife, we don't want to cook much anymore.

I do maintain a weight that is consistent, but within a ten-pound range, which I know is a lot, but that's where I am in life. Never too heavy, but never too thin. My doctor says I am in good shape for a seventy-three-year-old man. I take that as a win!

I often think I feed Miss Betty better than myself because I select her food and have it ready to go each day.

For myself, I will buy some things from the grocery store, but never full meals. I usually purchase some meats, vegetables, fruit, bread, milk, and crackers.

I am currently in the middle of a three-month attempt to not eat sugar. I am not completely sugar-free, because sugar is everywhere, but I am trying to avoid sugar.

It's going pretty well so far, but I have a way to go. We'll see how it works out.

Miss Betty does not have to worry about this, because I do not feed her any sugar.

She is my responsibility, and I take that seriously. Her health is my main job in caring for her.

We all eat every day, and some of us are strict when it comes to food. People are vegan, vegetarians, and all sorts of different foodies. I go by the "moderation" method, in which I can and want to eat all types of food—high-end food, fast food, tasty food, and everything in between. Just not too much of any one type of food. It has worked well for me. I hope you eat food with delight and try all types of food.

Chapter 28

SANCTUARY

To me, a sanctuary is a place where I am comfortable. I can completely relax and recharge my batteries. I think we all need this, considering the fast-paced and competitive world we live in.

When we got Miss Betty, we lived in Carmel, California. I was retired, and my office was the place where I could close the arched glass doors and close off the world for a bit—a place where I could think, read, and write. A sanctuary. I could watch people stroll by on their way to and from the beach. An observer without interaction, watching the village I lived in go about their daily walks.

Miss Betty had a fluffy blanket in there and would lay around and enjoy herself in that room—her sanctuary. We were both in our relaxing place when those doors closed.

Then we moved to a new location in the Sierra Nevada in 2021, and we needed to discover and create our new sanctuary.

Miss Betty and I required a place where we could be alone with each other, where time did not exist, and where the world slowed down to almost a stop.

To us, this new house was full of opportunity, and with my wife, we created not just one but several places we could call a sanctuary.

I have an office where I can write, read, and create. This "office" has two glass doors I can use to close off the rest of the house, yet I can look out the glass doors toward the back of the house, which has a view of the Reno Valley.

Miss Betty has her fluffy blanket and is comfortably sleeping as I write this chapter.

We also have three other areas that act as sanctuaries: The master bedroom, where at the end of the bed we have a small sofa that Miss Betty can rest on while I sit in the two chairs that we installed to let me read and enjoy quiet time. I can close the doors and be walled off from any commotion in the house. I sit and can look at the Reno Valley through a very large glass window. I can see but not hear the freeway in the distance, with cars speeding somewhere, going to important destinations. I can see the international airport, where silent airplanes take off and land. Miss Betty can get on her tippy-toes and look into the backyard from the windowsill. This is a wonderful space, and often when I am looking for Miss Betty in the late evening, she is resting by herself on the sofa—her sanctuary when she needs it.

We also have a living room, where we have two chairs that swivel and can face the backyard and all the buildings, freeway, and airport located in the valley. The chairs also face the front door, and Miss Betty and I can sit in each chair right next to each other. She is not supposed to sit on the furniture, but in this case, we allow it. She sits with me as I read the paper, a book, or make notes for a future writing project. When I am busy, I can look over and see Miss Betty resting, or should I say sleeping, on the comfortable chairs.

This house suits us well, and we have lots of individual areas to rest and relax.

We have found sanctuary spaces, but we also know we need these relaxing areas to recharge, to think without distractions, to enjoy the quiet that sanctuary affords us.

I think we all need a place to hide away, to be by ourselves, and to replenish our spirit—a place all ours for a time. Others can use the same space at different times for their quiet time or for the intended purpose. We all need our body and soul to feel refreshed. I hope that you who are reading this have a spot or spots you can us to refresh yourself. If not, find that space. Find that area in your lives where everything is—no judgment, no fears, a place to think, a place to enjoy the life you are living. You will live a longer life having a sanctuary.

Chapter 29

CATS

My daughter, Krista; my son, Joel; and my sister, Nancy each have two cats. Krista has Tahoe and Jewel, Joel has Finnigan and Isabel, and Nancy has Poppy and Lola.

They love their cats, and the cats bring them joy every day. Now, I don't mind cats and have had a few as my kids were growing up. We had Sally and Hobbs, and they were fine cats. They lived outdoors as much as indoors. We fed them and took care of them, but they were fiercely independent.

Krista, Joel, and Nancy all have indoor cats, and they are comforted by their pets. The cats are life in the house. They are company, and they cuddle together and are a source of pride for each of them.

I like their cats and have nothing bad to say about them. But they are not dogs.

Dogs are a different level of pet and companion. You take dogs for a walk. You don't take cats for a walk. Of course, you can, but most people don't. My son, Joel, took his two cats out for a walk when he lived in San Francisco. They were each on a leash, and the sight must have been hilarious—a big man walking these two scrawny little cats "on a leash."

Not a good look.

I take my two dogs out for a walk on a leash, and everything looks normal. I look like many people all over the world walking their dogs.

Uncle Frank and Miss Betty are indoor dogs, but they can spend quite a bit of time in our fenced-in backyard or our front courtyard area.

As long as they are contained, I do not worry about the dogs, and they can spend as much time as they want outdoors unsupervised.

Meanwhile, cats cannot be trusted to stay in a yard, even if it is fenced, because a fence is not a deterrent to cats.

They can be outdoors as long as Krista, Joel, and Nancy are around them, and only for a short time.

My other daughter, Holly, has a dog, Roxy, who Uncle Frank and Miss Betty love. They can't wait to play with each other. They enjoy their time together and cry when we have to leave.

On the other hand, Uncle Frank and Miss Betty are in fear of Finnigan and Isabel. When they go over to Joel's house, the first few minutes are pure terror, until the cats realize the dogs mean no harm, but the dogs stay on alert the entire time they are there. They are always happy to leave.

Dogs and cats are very different from each other for a variety of reasons, but they all bring comfort to our lives. They are fun to interact with and to have something in the house that needs our love and attention. They give love back in bucketfuls, and our world would be grayer without them.

I am always sad to leave my dogs and always happy to return home to them. Miss Betty is at my feet as I write this, and Uncle Frank is laying on his side in the sun, taking a nap. This is their heaven on earth, and I am proud to have them. They make my life better. I have love to give, and I enjoy the love they give me back. A lot of work? Yes, but work that I happily give and give with love.

We all need pets in our lives. Some cannot have pets around for a variety of reasons, but those who do are in a warmer place in life. Being retired with pets is the best. It is hard to have a job and leave your pets all day as you work. Being home with your pets is the best. Even when we leave for a vacation and get a pet sitter, we know we will return home to love and a lot of licks.

Chapter 30

SLICE OF LIFE

What's to become of us? Where will we end up? What does the future hold for Miss Betty? What does the future look like for my children? Where will this house end up? What will become of my wife and me?

The one thing I have learned with certainty is that all that we have and all that we hold special is temporary.

We live this life that we seem to think is a long life. But is it really? I am seventy-three years old as I write this in 2023. If I live another fifteen years, that will be eighty-eight. That seems like a long life, a lot of time. But is it? Eighty-eight years is but a small fraction of how long the earth has been around and how long humans have been on earth.

If my life span is 1950 to 2038, what does that represent? I always laughed that all your living and life occur at that small dash between the dates. What was my life? Did I enjoy it? Did I laugh and cry? Did I feel the thrill of life? Did I experience the pain? Did I experience love?

These are questions we all must face when the end of life is near.

The *slice* of time we are around and all the life that surrounds us during that time is what we call life.

I am surrounded by family and friends and, of course, Miss Betty. These are all things that touched me during my *slice* of life.

My children will grow older and face the same questions. Their children will be the engine that moves life forward. There will be other dogs in the future for other people. But Miss Betty is my dog in the time that I live. Writing this book about her and our daily lives will prolong our lives to a future that we will not participate in. Books have a way of keeping that *slice* of life around for future generations to read.

All that I see on my desk as I write will either be gone, recycled, or repurposed. Any money I have will be gone; my precious materialistic possessions in life will be gone. Where, I don't know, and will never know.

With that in mind, it is important to not put too much effort into *things* that will end up in a location you have no control over.

Some of these things do bring you satisfaction during your life. I look at a bottle of Cakebread wine on my shelf that states I came in first place, along with my wife and another couple, in a golf tournament in Pinehurst, North Carolina. Woo-hoo! That was so special, yet it is only special to me. When I am gone, it may be of interest to my children, but not beyond that.

I love the life I live because I want to love it. I put effort into things that make my life interesting. I look for the good in things, even with all the negativity in the world. I try to help where I can to make things better. I provide funds to those who I think will make a difference. I contribute time, effort, and money to causes I hold dear.

As I grow older, I am paring down things I have and giving things away to causes and people who I think will continue to put value into those things. Sometimes it's not a monetary value but a mental value.

I don't know what the future holds, but I do know I will put effort and love into all those who have touched my life. Miss Betty will be loved through all the time she has left with me. I will let the people around me know they are valued in my life. I will call, email, and text them notes to let them know I care and am thinking about them. I will cherish all the relationships I have, and Miss Betty and I will live out our lives as best we can.

The old song goes, "What will be will be. The future's not mine to see," and that is true for all of us. I sure did not live the life I had planned. But can you really plan a life? All types of adjustments are made, until the clear path becomes a winding, meandering road. That is why we are told to "enjoy the journey." I hope your life is an interesting journey. Miss Betty and I are traveling our road, and what will be will be.

ABOUT THE AUTHOR

Don Rose is a United States Army veteran and a graduate of the University of California, Berkeley. He is an artist, author, and retired landscape architect. Don lives in the Sierra Nevada mountains with his wife, Jenny, and their wonderful dogs, Uncle Frank and Miss Betty.

Afternoons with Miss Betty is Don's sixth book. Other books by Don Rose include:

When the Day Ends . . . and Dreams Begin . . .

When the Day Ends . . . and Dreams Begin . . . 2

When the Day Ends . . . and Dreams Begin . . . 3

AMAZING Adventures of Young SuperHeroes

Mornings with Uncle Frank